"With years of experience and a depth of biblical understanding, Jim Croft has brought us a jewel in his book Invisible Enemies. Dispelling myths and enlightening the reader with truth, you will be armed for battle to conquer your personal enemy and come out on the other side a victor and not a victim. I applaud Jim Croft for his work of excellence! Well done!"

James W. Goll, founder, Encounters Network and
Prayer Storm International; author, *The Seer,*
The Lost Art of Intercession, The Coming Israel
Awakening and many others

"I met Jim Croft in 1972 while he was helping a professor get free from life-long demonic oppressions. Before my very eyes I saw that man set free. Jim Croft and I have been close friends and associates ever since. I can testify that God has used him powerfully in the deliverance ministry for more than forty years. All that gleaned knowledge he has compacted into this book. When he shares about 'invisible enemies,' there is no one I know better qualified to teach on this vital subject. With scriptural balance, unique insights, loving grace and distinct humor, Jim Croft has presented us with a precious gem that will enlighten and guide all believers for the coming battles against darkness and advance the Kingdom of God."

Dr. Mahesh Chavda, co-founder and senior pastor,
All Nations Church (Charlotte, NC, and Atlanta, GA);
coauthor, *Getting to Know the Holy Spirit* and *Only Love*
Can Make a Miracle; www.maheshchavda.com

INVISIBLE
ENEMIES

INVISIBLE ENEMIES

JIM CROFT

Chosen
a division of Baker Publishing Group
www.ChosenBooks.com

Published by Chosen Books
11400 Hampshire Avenue South
Bloomington, Minnesota 55438

Chosen Books is a division of
Baker Publishing Group, Grand Rapids, Michigan.

Printed in the United States of America

Library of Congress Cataloging-in-Publication Data

Croft, Jim.
    Invisible enemies : how to recognize and defeat demons / Jim Croft ; foreword by Dick Leggatt.
       p. cm.
    Includes index.
    ISBN 978-0-8007-9507-8 (pbk. : alk. paper) 1. Exorcism. 2. Spiritual warfare. I. Title.

BV873.E8C76   2011
235'.4—dc22

2011002691

Contents

Foreword by Dick Leggatt   9

Acknowledgments   13

Introduction   15

Part 1   Facing Reality

  1. The Truth about Deliverance   21

  2. Transforming Encounters   29

  3. Proved Wrong, and Glad of It   35

  4. Early Attempts at Deliverance   43

  5. Learning about Satan's Kingdom   51

  6. The Christian Dilemma   63

  7. Jesus and the Exorcists   75

  8. Initial Steps to Freedom   93

  9. Self-Deliverance   103

Part 2   The Next Step toward Freedom

  10. Biblical Truth and Human Understanding   117

11. Separating Ministry Chaff from Wheat   123

12. Deliverance in Conjunction with Other Biblical Practices   135

Part 3   Deeper into Deliverance

13. Obliterating Demonic Strongholds in Your Mind   147

14. Dealing with Denouncements and Vows   161

15. Manipulation and Soul Ties   173

16. Breaking the Power of Sex Perversions   179

17. Dealing with Spirits of Infirmity   187

18. Expelling Home-Wrecking Demons   195

19. Deliverance from the Powers of Iniquity   201

20. Battling Spirits of Antichrist   209

21. Guidelines for Helping Others   219

Epilogue: The Challenge of Commitment   227

Appendix: Ministry Resource Guide   229

Index   233

Foreword

I'm honored to write the foreword for this book authored by my good friend and colleague Jim Croft. We have known one another since 1975. Our families have enjoyed time as friends, times of ministry, times of worship and prayer, times of collaboration in writing and editorial work, times of recreation. All this is to say that I consider it a great privilege to know Jim and his unique ways.

The familiar saying, "They broke the mold after he was created," comes strongly to mind. Jim is unique in his transparency regarding his own life and ministry. He is unique in his amazing, offbeat sense of humor, his honesty and candor, and his impact upon so many sectors of the Body of Christ.

Jim is especially unique in his God-given calling to the vital area of spiritual warfare and the deliverance ministry. This book, reflecting all those areas of uniqueness, will greatly enhance your understanding of the subject of deliverance.

I believe this book will benefit you in three important areas of your Christian experience.

Regarding the Topic of Demons

First, it will help you develop a normal, matter-of-fact attitude toward deliverance and demons.

This book provides a practical and balanced look at the reality of spiritual warfare in the Christian life. Jim's down-to-earth approach to dealing with potential demonic influence in our own lives, in others and in our society is candid and refreshing. Unfortunately, the Church has tended to marginalize this important biblical issue. We have ignored the elephant in the room. We know it's there; we just refuse to talk about it.

If we were absolutely honest, we would freely admit that we grapple with serious problems in our lives. For many, those problems go well beyond the boundaries of routine character flaws. Those are the ones we don't talk about in polite company—the compulsive and at times uncontrollable matters that erupt in private; the secret sexual preoccupations that are embarrassing even to our own sensibilities; the obsessive/compulsive behaviors that we wish we could control or eliminate, but cannot.

Certainly, most problems we exhibit are the routine result of faulty character traits, downright orneriness or a myriad of basic human weaknesses. Honesty demands, however, that we also acknowledge that other category of problems whose symptoms can be telltale signs of demonic influence in our lives.

The very mention of the word *demon* in polite company tends to thrust most of us into the realm of denial or panic. "You mean to tell me you believe I have a demon at work in my personality?" The answer is yes; demons are simply facts of life that every person experiences at some level. As you read Jim's book, you will discover how normal this entire phenomenon and process can be.

The Scriptures Jim explores in this book attest that it was a normal part of life in Jesus' time as well. In scriptural accounts of Jesus' ministry, He would regularly heal a person of a physical malady through prayer. Other times He would cast out the demon causing the malady. In both approaches, the result was the same: complete healing and restoration. Jesus made no distinction between healing and deliverance. He employed both with equanimity and balance.

And when Jesus was confronting a demonic presence rather than a physical ailment, He did not react with surprise or anxiety, but was steady and controlled. For Jesus, it was nothing out of the ordinary. And it should not be for us either.

How then do we develop the unflappable attitude toward demons that Jesus exhibited? Jim shares very transparently about personal experiences that helped him understand demonic opposition as a fairly common occurrence in Christian experience. He also shares substantive teaching to provide a clear, expansive picture of the entire topic of spiritual warfare. But first and foremost, what Jim writes can help to produce your first benefit from this book: developing a well-adjusted, matter-of-fact attitude toward deliverance and demons.

Regarding Your Own Need for Deliverance

The second benefit is learning how to be set free from the effects of your own "invisible enemies" that have pushed you around for far too long. Writing about his own experiences and offering solid teaching, Jim provides practical means for us to get free and stay free.

Much could be said about this second benefit, but bottom line, Jim provides enough enlightened instruction in this book to deal with demonic oppression in your own life. And that experience will lead to the third benefit.

Regarding Helping Others Find Freedom

Far more people struggle with demonic torment than there are qualified people to help them out of that torment. Almost daily at Derek Prince Ministries, we receive desperate calls for help from people trying to get free from some type of demonic oppression. They ask for referrals to someone in their area who is able to minister to their needs as Jim's mentor, Derek Prince, would have ministered.

Far too often, our response is that we are not aware of anyone in their area who is knowledgeable or experienced in the matter of casting out demons. The third benefit is Jim's purpose in this book: to educate, train and inspire others to carry on the ministry he, his mentors and other servants of the Lord have carried on for many decades.

The good news is that such knowledge and skills concerning deliverance are attainable for you. In fact, by the time you finish reading this book, you should be prepared to step out prayerfully to help yourself and others who may seek freedom from demonic oppression. And in our society today, the extensive preoccupation we are seeing with occult themes may end up requiring a whole army of compassionate people to respond to what could become an overwhelming need.

It is abundantly clear from prophetic Scriptures and the account of Jesus' life on earth that He came to set the captives free. He gave us that same mandate and commission. Are you ready to fulfill it?

If you have answered yes to that challenge, the best first step in answering the call is simply to read and digest the truths Jim Croft spells out in this book. Then step up to the line, as Jim's ending section directs, and offer yourself completely to the Lord Jesus Christ.

Present yourself to Him, and ask to receive His cleansing ministry in your own life.

Then, present yourself to Him to carry on, by His power and grace (using the tools you have received in this book), His ministry to set the captives free.

DICK LEGGATT
PRESIDENT, DEREK PRINCE MINISTRIES—USA

Acknowledgments

I would like to thank Dick Leggatt for serving as my in-house editor. His fine-tuning skills are without equal. I am also very grateful for Dennis Williams's diligence in proofreading the numerous drafts of each chapter. Both Dick and Dennis made tremendous sacrifices of their time and energies to see to it that the manuscript was delivered in a timely manner. Bless you, dear brothers.

Introduction

Jesus and His team of disciples traveled through the cities of Israel, performing healing miracles and expelling demons from people everywhere they went (see Mark 1:23–27).

The majority of those to whom they ministered were not from the dregs of society. Most, by all outward appearances, led reputable lives—doing their best to provide for their families and live responsibly according to the Law of Moses. Yet, like many present-day, upstanding, responsible people, they had secret struggles that seemed beyond their control—until the light of Jesus drove the invisible enemies from their lives.

Demonic Presences in Our Day

Jesus cast evil spirits out of people because that is precisely what they needed. Any suggestion that biblical deliverance is simply archaic terminology for addressing the psychological anomalies of the day is off base. Even today we use Greek root words to define most modern-day disorders. If counseling therapy is what Jesus did for people, the language of His era would have been adequate to define it precisely in those terms. The Bible offers no such notions.

Modern man continues to struggle with the mysteries of human personality and with the bodily afflictions so many suffer. We recognize, with gratitude, that partial answers have been found through psychological counseling and medical science breakthroughs. But in spite of tireless efforts many lives remain unchanged. We need to face reality—a Bible-based Christian concept: Evil spirits afflict the personalities and bodies of people today just as they did two thousand years ago. Those invisible enemies need to be expelled.

Jesus came preaching peace to those who were near and to those who were "afar off" (Ephesians 2:17). Our birth in this generation qualifies us as ones who are in the "afar off" category; therefore, it also qualifies us for the peace Jesus offers.

Peace means literally "freedom from molestation to the extent that one can enjoy an untroubled, undisturbed sense of ongoing well-being." That is also a wonderful description of an effective deliverance from demonic spirits.

The Purpose of This Book

Perhaps you are not a churchgoer, but are suspicious that demonic powers might be manipulating some aspect of your personality. Don't worry about any affiliations with organized religion. Jesus wants you free. The Bible states that those who call upon the name of the Lord will be saved. One of the definitions for *saved* is "deliverance." If you are drowning, the Lord is willing to throw you a lifeline of deliverance. Once you are safely onboard the "Power of His Name" ship, there will be plenty of time to work out the details about how to express your faith in Jesus.

In other words, whether you are completely converted to Christ or standoffish about matters of religion, the Lord's will for you is liberation from all of the schemes of the devil. And that is the purpose for which this book was written.

It is designed to alert you to the unseen spiritual activities of invisible enemies. And it will equip you to deal with those forces just as Jesus did, bringing you into liberty and peace.

With an abundance of personal stories and experiences, we will explore the unseen reality that most of us deal with every day from the demonic realm. The Bible gives us much to ponder about Satan's evil kingdom. That knowledge will help us demythologize the subject of deliverance and demons and approach it effectively.

We will also answer some hard questions: Can a Christian really "have a demon"? How is that possible? We will cut through the Hollywood stereotypes of what commonly happens when people are delivered from evil spirits, and expose some of the aberrant methodologies that have evolved, countering them with Bible-based techniques.

Now, we will discuss this in detail later, but let me state it clearly here so that you have no question: *A Christian cannot be demon possessed in the sense of total ownership and control. Believers are owned by Jesus, and the spiritually minded submit their lives to the precepts of God's Word and to the control of the Holy Spirit.* As we will see, however, demons can oppose, torment, molest and invade aspects of the personalities and health of these same individuals.

Once we have a solid foundation for understanding the workings of these evil beings, we will look at deliverance techniques that are biblical and effective. This book will teach you how to be set free and how to maintain your freedom—even in the face of the growing influence in the world today of the antichrist spirit.

The book will close with a challenge for you, once free, to equip yourself to assist others in winning their own battles with demonic powers.

Information about the enemy and how to defeat him is not hidden from us. God intends for us to know the peace available in the power of the name of Jesus. Let's begin our study, then, to understand the ways He wants us to defeat these uninvited evil spirits, and walk boldly into our freedom.

PART ONE

Facing Reality

Many contemporary Christians believe that the New Testament accounts of Jesus and the early believers casting out demons are true—for that day and age. And some may go so far as to see these deliverances as archaic predecessors of present-day counseling. If demons do exist, they are likely restricted to idolatrous tribes in foreign lands and perhaps to a few cases of extreme mental instability.

As a result of not being informed about the ongoing existence and purpose of spirits spoken about in the Scriptures, they have no context for believing that demonic activity could be remotely applicable to their problems. The blindness is costly.

If we negate the possibility of demonic influence, we must attribute our inner struggles and the dark side of our behavior to our failure to cultivate godly character. The response for Christians is to intensify spiritual regimens of Bible reading, prayer and church activities as corrective measures.

But when demons are the root issue, those remedies provide little more than temporary relief for sinful behavior and guilt. The demon-driven aspects of the problems usually remain.

In Part 1, we will discover that the answer for which so many long is found in the deliverance ministries of Jesus and the early Church apostles. Vile entities called demons do exist. It is not unusual for them to foster and feed every kind of misery, from relational disharmony to sickness and even death. We will learn how evil spirits torment individuals, and how to discern if you would benefit from deliverance ministry.

1

The Truth about Deliverance

One of the primary objectives of demonic influence upon human personalities and physical bodies is to complicate the lives of people whom the enemy is targeting. The devil, who is commander-in-chief of all demonic forces, would prefer to attack God directly. Because he cannot do so, he opts to attack the crown of God's creation—mankind.

The devil uses evil spirits of varying strengths and types. All have specific destructive inclinations, and they yearn to manifest them in flesh-and-blood hosts. Spirits operate in a number of ways to express their cruel designs. Producing misery is their favorite dish, and they choose from a broad menu: marital disharmony, emotional upheaval, mental disorders, bizarre sexual appetites, verbal and physical abuse, economic frustration, physical infirmity. Basically, any malady capable of producing heartache may have demonic origins.

But it is also true that not every problem automatically comes from a demonic source. Sporadic episodes of depression, anger, anxiety and other emotional problems, for instance, can be the result of abusive parenting and adulthood traumas. Human pride and guilt about habitual sins, along with hormonal imbalances, can also incite emotional stress.

Along the same lines, not every activity that seems to endorse the satanic agenda is a guarantee of demonic infestation. Occult involvement is a common vehicle for demonic infiltration, and children and adults who become preoccupied with occult practices or articles place themselves at high risk. But a child's watching an occasional spooky film or reading Harry Potter books or dressing up for Halloween does not automatically doom him or her to be on the receiving end of a spirit of witchcraft. (We will discuss this in more depth later, but let me note here that parents who are too stringent in their concerns about their kids being contaminated may win that skirmish, but ultimately discover they have lost the war. Legalism has a way of producing rebels.)

Evil spirits are crafty opportunists, granted, but human beings have an innate power second only to the Trinity: It is the inner spirit, which is the essence of each individual's personal identification as a living being. The Scriptures depict the spirit of each person as the guardian of his or her inner walled city and interior house (see Proverbs 25:28). Some people who are very strong in character and spirit can defend their inner territories, without necessarily concentrating on doing so every minute of every day.

Put simply, we have the resources to be in charge of our behavior. Why, then, do so many people struggle with issues that indicate the presence of demons? Here is the problem: Most people are not as adept at keeping their city walls intact as their pride might lead them to believe. Pride, as Scripture so clearly states, often precedes destruction (see Proverbs 16:18). It weakens city walls and can cause an individual's inner spirit to overlook the approach of enemies wanting to break into his house (see Matthew 12:43–45).

Most any enemy can jump through city walls that have breaks and gaps in them. It is a foolish gamble for anyone to override his conscience and engage in behavior that flagrantly defies scriptural prohibitions—such as delving into occult practice or even exploration. People who do so are unwittingly weakening their own inner defenses. It is an open invitation to evil spirits stronger than the person's area of weakness; demons are waiting to pounce.

To further complicate the problem, it is not always sin that attracts invasion. Although it seems hard to believe, innocent people can become repositories for evil spirits. Those who have been worn down by traumatic events that are no fault of their own, for instance, often have weakened city walls. While the demons cannot entirely "possess" or "own" any individuals who profess the name of Jesus, evil spirits, nonetheless, can reside in and influence many aspects of their lives.

This is what happened to one of my daughters when my wife, Prudence, almost died during her birth. I tell her story below. This particular situation was not occasioned by anything we or our infant daughter had done wrong. Beautiful roses can be blighted. Well-behaved dogs can get fleas. Innocent lambs can be infested with parasites. And precious children can become disease-ridden.

Satan's hordes do not respect human boundaries, but they can be ejected from our lives. Recognition of their presence and application of the power transmitted to believers by the resurrection of Jesus can provide deliverance and safe haven.

Our Daughter's Deliverance

Our two oldest daughters, Kari and Sharon, were born with serious asthmatic conditions. Regular medical treatments kept them functional. Then, shortly after I became a Christian, Prudence and I prayed for the Lord to heal them. We thank God that He erased every symptom from their lives.

The situation with our third daughter, Holly, was quite different. She was saved and filled with the Holy Spirit at an early age. Nonetheless, her health history and certain aspects of her behavior puzzled us. None of the symptoms she exhibited was alleviated until she received deliverance ministry at the age of five.

Holly had a stubborn streak that was uncharacteristic of her siblings. In the area of health, she did not respond to prayers for healing in the same way as her older sisters. For instance, all of the girls would catch the sniffles and we would pray for them simultaneously. Invariably, Kari and Sharon would be completely healed within several hours of our prayer. Or they would recover fully within a day or two at most. But that was never the case with Holly. Her condition always seemed to worsen.

For several years, it seemed we were taking Holly weekly to the doctor's office. No matter how minor the initial symptoms were, they would escalate rapidly into serious complications. Extended periods of sickness made her weak and whiny.

Prudence and I grew weary from concern, sleepless nights and enormous medical bills. Above all, we were both disappointed by the fruitlessness of our prayers for her healing. And we were mystified that our every attempt to help her cultivate a more agreeable attitude failed.

Helpful Discernment

One evening, Prudence came to me full of optimism. She told me that while she had been praying about Holly's condition, the Lord had given her a spiritual revelation. He had reminded Prudence of several pertinent facts. Holly had been born under traumatic circumstances. First, she was over a month premature. After her birth, she was hospitalized with a life-threatening respiratory ailment. In addition, after the delivery, Prudence had approached death's door due to massive hemorrhaging.

As she shared all this with me, Prudence beamed with confidence. She was certain she had heard from the Lord.

"Jim, God gave me a vision of demons of infirmity and death entering Holly during her birth. The reason she doesn't respond when we anoint her with oil and pray is because we are dealing with evil spirits, not routine sicknesses. We must take authority over them and cast them out in the name of Jesus."

As Prudence spoke, something like inner agreement clicked within my spirit. I knew that what she was saying was absolutely on-target. We were very familiar with seeing people liberated from evil spirits, and I was filled with hope sensing that we were on the brink of a breakthrough for our child. Prudence and I both agreed that the best approach was immediate action. So we asked Holly to sit down with us in the living room for a talk.

As we all sat on the couch together, I explained to her as best I could what we were going to do. "Honey," I said gently, "God has shown Mommy that there are some naughty spirits inside of you that make you sick all of the time. Daddy is going to tell them to come out of you in Jesus' name."

Holly looked a little unsure. Prudence slipped her arm around Holly's waist, and I continued to explain.

"I'm going to speak very firmly to those nasty spirits while I'm looking at you, and I'm going to tell them to come out. It may sound as though I'm angry, but I'm not mad at you. We know you want to be a healthy and good girl. I am mad at the devil and the mean spirits that make you sick."

Holly nodded at this point, seeming to understand, so I went on.

"I want you to look straight at me. When I tell the spirits to leave, you just open your mouth a little bit and breathe them out through your mouth."

At that, Holly again looked puzzled. I thought to remind her of her experience of being baptized with the Holy Spirit. "Holly, do you remember how you breathed in the good Holy Spirit?" She nodded. "Well, after I tell the bad spirits to come out of you, I want you to huff and puff them out so the good Holy Spirit will have more room."

A Little "Corpse"

What happened next was astonishing. As soon as I commanded the demons of death and infirmity to come out of my daughter, she gagged as though something were lodged in her throat.

Her tiny frame shook convulsively. Her face went ashen white, and her eyes rolled back into her head with only the whites showing. She then collapsed on the couch as though dead. In fact, she actually looked like a little corpse. But rather than panicking in concern at her appearance, I picked her up and began to laugh and sing and thank the Lord. I knew the troubling entities were gone.

Suddenly, Holly opened her eyes and smiled shyly up at me. She looked different. Her face was bright and her eyes were clear. Prudence and I knew in that moment that Holly was free from the chronic sicknesses and demonic forces that had attempted to snatch her life.

After that time of prayer on the couch, Holly did not have to visit a doctor's office, nor did she experience any type of sickness again, for at least five years. At the time of this writing, she is 43 years of age, the happily married mother of two. To this very day, Holly remains in vibrant health.

There was another unexpected benefit of Holly's deliverance session. Even though I had not specifically addressed her behavioral problems, we saw a dramatic change in her attitude. She became as cooperative as our other daughters. Apparently, as the power of the Holy Spirit freed Holly from demons of ill health, the spirit of stubbornness also gave up and left.

Trekking Onward

Learning from that experience that demons are opportunists helped me see the truth and clarity of what the Bible says about this amazing and powerful ministry of deliverance. Abiding fruit can only be produced by principles and practices soundly based on the Word of God.

I would like to begin our journey with my own experience of learning about deliverance. In the next three chapters, I tell the story of my recognition of and liberation from the invisible enemies I had been dealing with most of my life. Your story may be similar or quite different. But the outcome, freedom, awaits you as well.

2

Transforming Encounters

At the age of 25, I had not yet entered the full-time ministry that has
been my career for the past three decades. At that time, I was a sales
representative for a shoe manufacturer, a position requiring travel to
stores in the southern states. During a call on the shoe department
of a major Birmingham, Alabama, department store, I learned while
talking with the store's shoe buyer, Michael, that his marriage was
in trouble.

Initially, I spoke to Michael about how prayer could heal marriages. My objective was to determine whether or not he had a personal
relationship with Christ. He was polite, but let me know he did not
enjoy chitchat about personal spiritual matters.

Rather bluntly, Michael encouraged me to go and talk instead
to his buddy Ted, the toy buyer, with this sarcastic parting remark:
"Yeah, Ted is a Bible-banger like you." Seeing that I was getting
nowhere with Michael, I asked directions to Ted's office, thinking
that Ted and I might be able to pray together for Michael's marriage.

A Surprising Topic of Conversation

Arriving at Ted's office, I introduced myself. When he heard that I was a believer, he shouted hallelujah with a zeal that I found unsettling.

"I just talked with Michael, your shoe buyer," I offered. "His marriage seems to be in trouble, and I thought maybe we might pray together for him."

A moment later, I realized that it was not going to be that simple. I got a lot more than the quick prayer of agreement I had anticipated. Instead of praying, Ted not only began to ramble, but he spoke like a fanatic about demons being at the root of Michael's troubles.

"You know, Jim, demons torment people today just as they did back in Bible times. Seriously! And there is a British fellow in town right now who is a Bible teacher and an expert on demonology. You ought to go hear him while you're here on business."

At that point, I was looking for the nearest exit. But Ted kept talking, trying to persuade me to go hear this Cambridge-educated theologian, an expert in the biblical languages of antiquity who "actually casts demons out of people."

Frankly, I could not understand how we had gotten on this strange topic. I had no interest whatsoever in learning about casting demons out of people. But whenever I tried to get the conversation back on track, nothing registered with Ted. He refused to let up about the topic of demons, and I was getting increasingly uncomfortable and exasperated.

"Jim, I can't tell you how exciting it is to see people set free— people who had no idea they were being influenced by an evil spirit. They are getting released from anger, anxiety, depression, diseases— even lust."

Suddenly, Ted uttered a word I had never heard spoken in polite company. With excitement in his voice, he said, "You know, I was delivered from a spirit of masturbation that had hounded me from my teens!"

With his southern drawl, Ted accentuated every syllable. I winced in embarrassment, not only at his lack of propriety, but also at the realization that he was hitting way too close to home. A shameful alarm was starting to ring within me, but I shrugged off the impression. What nerve he had! How could he speak of such a disdainful personal problem to someone he had just met?

Apparently, Ted finally read my facial expression and body language. "Well, okay, Jim. You probably have to take off, and I guess you want to pray for Michael." Dutifully, he bowed his head and prayed for Michael's marriage.

"Amen," I said quickly, relieved that the demon talk had finally ended.

As I stood and reached out my hand to shake good-bye, he slipped a yellow promotional flyer into it.

Staying Away from the Fray

Once outside his office door, I glanced at the flyer. It was an advertisement for a deliverance seminar sponsored by the Full Gospel Business Men's Fellowship International (FGBMFI) and featuring the ministry of British theologian Derek Prince. Disgusted at the thought, I crammed the flyer into my suit pocket.

Undergirded by the fact that at least we had prayed for Michael, I hastened back to the shoe buyer's office to speak with him further about salvation. Michael met me with an impish grin.

"Ted's quite a guy, isn't he?" Michael said. Before answering, I mentally ran through a list of definitions of *quite a guy* for which Ted might qualify. For me, he fell somewhere between a hyper-religious flake and a total jerk. But rather than make an uncharitable assessment of Ted, I said simply, "Yes, indeed. Ted is quite a guy."

Michael and I took a few minutes to talk further, and although he did not ask Jesus to become his Savior, he did allow me to pray for his family, and for harmony to return to his relationship with his wife.

Back at my hotel room, I changed into casual clothes before

going down to supper. While hanging up my suit coat, I noticed the yellow flyer in my pocket. I ripped it into shreds and threw it into the trash can.

As it turned out, the demonology seminar was being held at that very hotel. When I settled into a seat at a restaurant on the mezzanine level, the meeting had just started. As I ate, I could hear the singing of unfamiliar choruses coming from the ballroom below. Occasionally, I caught bits of exuberant testimonies about the power of the Holy Spirit.

All through my meal, a battle was in progress between my heart and mind. My heart was quietly urging me to attend the meeting. My mind was countering with vehement reasons to stay put.

You don't want to go in there, my reasoning faculties said. *You know Ted is there, and he will scope you out and pounce on you like a cat after a canary. For crying out loud, those are Pentecostals in that meeting! You can hear them hooting it up all the way up here in the restaurant. How would it look for you, a respectable Southern Baptist and a well-known spokesman for Gideon International, to walk into such a meeting?*

The thought of a tarnished reputation was very convincing. My mind continued its rant. *You've been to scores of churches in this region giving your testimony about coming to Christ through a Gideon Bible placed in a hotel. It will all be spoiled if you join in with that bunch.*

Then the thought of chicanery rose: *Don't you realize that regardless of his pompous credentials, that Englishman is just another misdirected "Holy Roller" fanatic? He's probably a charlatan like all the rest—just in it for the money.*

Eventually, my mind won the battle. I returned to my hotel room after finishing dinner. As usual, I studied my Bible and prayed for my lost friends and the next day's calls. All the while, something or Someone within kept gently coaxing me to get down to that meeting.

But to my shame, my rebellion led me in a direction I loathed, one that had become a pattern in my sales travels. Once again, I soiled my conscience through sexual self-gratification. The routine was all too familiar. And once again, guilt battered me.

I knew all the Scriptures, especially the one in Matthew 5:28 that reminded me that my Lord considered even looking on a woman with lust as committing adultery. Logic dictated that my fantasizing about women accompanied by a sexual release made the offense even worse. I fell to my knees and repented for what seemed to be the millionth time. I then reached for my Bible to salve my conscience and eventually slipped into sleep with it in my hands.

Why My Battle Raged On

It was not until many months after the episode in Birmingham that I came to understand the process much better. Why had I been so repulsed by Ted's enthusiasm about deliverance from evil spirits? I realized that it was because I myself was dealing with unseen enemies.

My own personality had been infiltrated by evil spirits that definitely did not want me to go to that deliverance conference. Those demons knew that had I gone to the meeting, they might have lost their happy home. My mental accusations against Ted and my combative reasons for not attending the meeting that night were not entirely my own. Many were fueled by evil spirits inserting their thoughts into mine.

The phenomenon I just described is not unique to me. There are many good-natured people who have similarly hostile thoughts injected into their minds on a daily basis. Those people have genuinely good intentions. They long to have close friends, pleasant vocational environments and loving family relationships, but they often fail because they are plagued by critical thoughts that swim spontaneously through their cognitive processes. The malicious intent of that demonic activity is to incite arguments and to alienate their hosts from others and from any chance for harmonious living.

On the sexual side, the aberrant drives that people assume are just natural inclinations are nothing of the kind. Often, those thoughts and inclinations are the product of attacks from satanic entities that invaded their psyches during their formative years. These powers trash their God-given inhibitions, causing their consciences to become so calloused that they accept that which is unnatural and defiling as natural and harmless.

As it was with me, so it can be with many people of moral upright-ness. It is one thing for a hormone-invigorated teen to experiment with masturbation. It is quite another for a married person to disregard marriage vows by fantasizing about sexual escapades with members of the opposite sex. The solution for my unholy habit of sexual self-gratification was deliverance from the demon spawning it. Amazingly, when it happened, my release was instantaneous and permanent.

3

Proved Wrong, and Glad of It

It was my parents who introduced me to Don VanHoozier, the minister who helped to set me free. In turn, it was Pastor Don who got me connected with the ministry of Derek Prince, the Cambridge philosopher-turned-preacher who would soon hold such a valued place in my life.

At the time of my initial contact with Pastor Don, Prudence and I were living in Jackson, Mississippi, with our three young daughters. A fourth daughter, Rachel, came ten years later. Our family was very active in a local Southern Baptist church. My parents, who lived in Atlanta, Georgia, were godly, conservative evangelicals who attended a Presbyterian church that emphasized evangelism.

Everything was going along routinely until my mother got spiritually hungry for something more.

Some Renegade Baptists

One evening, my father called me with some rather startling news. He began by saying that my mother had hauled him to a meeting of the FGBMFI. To his shock (and awe), she had gone forward for prayer, seeking Holy Spirit baptism with the evidence of speaking in unknown tongues. He did what he imagined any respectable retired military officer and head of his conservative Christian household would do. He followed her politely to the altar, lifted her bodily from the waist and walked her off the premises.

Up to that point in their lives, both my father and mother believed that the gifts of the Holy Spirit had ceased during the first century. With that understanding firmly in place, my father felt that no wife of his should or would ever start dabbling in "Holy Roller" foolishness. What happened to my father later that night blew his theology to smithereens.

At about two in the morning, he was awakened from sleep by a voice. He sat up to see a bright light filling the room as my mother slumbered peacefully beside him. A voice spoke from the light and said something to this effect: *I now baptize you in My Spirit.* Dad instantly began to speak in a language he had never learned. The next morning, he could hardly get a word out in English as he told my mother what had occurred during the night.

Her reaction was twofold. Her first response was joy. Her second response was to scold my father for not waking her so she could have shared the experience. They were thus set on journeys near and far seeking the baptism with the Holy Spirit for my mother. Along the way they discovered delights from the Word of God to which they had previously been blind. Mom's search was satisfied when they visited High Point Southern Baptist Church in Macon, Georgia.

The phone call from my father that evening filled me with concern, as he and my mother took turns telling me about the wonders they had seen and experienced as they continued to attend the Baptist church in Georgia. They said that everyone, from the pastor to the janitor, had been blessed with gifts of the Spirit. They talked excitedly about people getting delivered from demons, prophesying and being healed of sicknesses.

Out of a deep sense of alarm (they had obviously gone off the deep end) I suggested that Prudence and the girls and I meet them at the church in Macon on the following Sunday. As I hung up the phone, I thought: *Southern Baptist church, my foot! In my estimation, that church is filled with nothing but renegades!*

I was determined to expose the fraud.

The Church in Macon

On the three-hundred-mile drive from Jackson, Mississippi, to Macon, Georgia, my mind defaulted into that same combative mode with my heart that I had experienced in Birmingham. A stream of testy, condescending remarks rushed into my mind. The scenes shifted from one scenario to the next as I anticipated how I would react in each event.

I had no clue, however, that the barrage of thoughts coming to me were actually instructions from demons that were working within me. I thought the vindictive put-downs were all coming from my marvelously astute doctrinal perspectives.

When Prudence and I and our girls entered the church in Macon with my parents, I discovered to my surprise that Pastor Don VanHoozier was a genuinely warm person. At our introduction, he brushed past my formal offer of a handshake and instead wrapped his long skinny arms around me.

I went stiff as a board, but he did not let me go. He rocked me like a child with his chin resting on the top of my head. "Oh, Jimmy, I'm so glad to meet you at last. Come on into my office and you can pray with my deacons before the service." I was embarrassed enough about being hugged by a beanstalk of a man for what seemed like an eternity. Now he wanted me to join him and his crew for prayer and go further out of my comfort zone. Before I could protest, I found myself standing in his office surrounded by six smiling men. I felt like a worm at a bird convention.

A short man who fit my perception of a redneck placed his hand on my head and began to speak. For a moment I grew tense, wondering if I would be subjected to their supposed gift of speaking in tongues that my parents had described. I relaxed. The language in which he spoke was not gibberish. My father had been stationed in Germany during my early teens, and I easily recognized that the deacon was speaking German. I was fascinated by the man's fluency: His speech had no hint of a rural Georgia drawl.

Just as he finished speaking, another man began to talk, interpreting for us the words just spoken in German. He told how God had called me from birth to be a Bible teacher, how I would travel the globe setting the captives free from demonic powers. I was stunned by the significance of his words. I was not familiar with what it meant to be a Bible teacher, and I had only budding perceptions of what "setting the captives free" might entail. Yet the words hit my heart with accuracy: God had clearly spoken to me, directing me into my life's calling.

As the prayer time ended, I was touched by a sense of God's power, but still cautious. I started to converse with those two men using the bit of German vocabulary at my command, but clearly neither of them understood a word I was saying.

Now I was utterly amazed. Had I actually been on the receiving end of the gifts in the Bible known as speaking in and interpreting tongues?

It was time for the morning service to begin and our little group parted. As I walked into the sanctuary, my heart acknowledged that the renegade Baptists were experiencing more of God than I was. And what was more, I suddenly knew I wanted what they had.

After the morning service, Prudence and I stayed for the evening service as well. Afterward, Prudence returned to our motel with the children, and I talked with Pastor Don late into the night. I had not told him anything about my personal problems. A few times during our talk together one of my carefully orchestrated arguments would raise its proud head. When that happened, he would just smile and gently disarm whatever I said with a prowess in the Scriptures like none I had ever witnessed.

As our conversation concluded and I rose to leave, eager to tell

Prudence all I had learned, Pastor Don asked if he could pray for me. Alarms went off in my head, all of them screaming for me to run out of the building. But this time my heart won, and I gave the pastor my consent. I was expecting a generic "bless-us-as-we-go-our-separate-ways" benediction. That was not even close to what happened.

My First Personal Deliverance

Pastor Don asked me to sit in a chair and he stood behind me. He thanked God for my life and for bringing us together. He then said something I had not ever heard in a prayer. "Father, in Jesus' name, I bind every evil force in the atmosphere around us and anything that might be complicating the life of this dear son of Yours."

Unknown to me, I was on the brink of getting demons expelled from me. He did not mention anything about demons or evil spirits. There was no shouting and by no means was it an aggressive ritual. Pastor Don had an unpretentious confidence in the anointed authority he possessed. More importantly, he somehow knew that the vile entities he was addressing were also aware of his authority.

As Pastor Don prayed for me, it was as though my sins and struggles were being broadcast into his thoughts from a direct spiritual wiretap of my conscience. He dealt with specific evil spirits in several ways. At times he called them "things" and at other times "powers." When doing so he would describe the particular activity of the demon, and then tell it to be gone from me. At other times he would identify a spirit by its particular function, and tell it to go in Jesus' name. It seemed evident that he was speaking to spiritual entities having faculties and personalities similar to those of humans.

"I order this thing that causes Jimmy to give harsh critical assessments of others to come out of him in Jesus' name. You powers that compel him to lie and to exaggerate, leave him now. Insecurity, the blood of the Lamb and the power of Jim's adoption into the family of God render your whispers null and void. Come out of him now in the matchless name of the Lord. From this moment forward, this sexual power that drives him to defile his sense of dignity as a recipient of God's grace is banished forever." Without question, the pastor was speaking to the spirit of masturbation that had been so disconcerting for me. It left. All of the spirits he commanded to depart did so.

I did not have any of the grotesque manifestations portrayed in the movie *The Exorcist*. I would estimate that I was liberated from at least five distinct evil spirits. As each one left, I felt a gentle lifting sensation in my abdominal area. Then I would either breathe out a little air as with a stifled burp or I would sigh with a yawn. I was hoping the minister would not think me rude or bored.

Pastor Don indicated the session was over by saying a hearty, joyful, "Amen!" Then he looked at me with one of the kindest expressions on his face that I had ever seen. "How are you doing, Jimmy?"

I responded, "To tell you the truth, I feel like a new man. Each time you prayed, I felt a lifting sensation in my gut. Were those sensations the demons you were calling out of me?"

"Yes, my boy," Pastor Don replied. "A lot of faithful saints are carrying around excess baggage they never knew existed. When the weight is off-loaded, their Christlike characters are liberated to shine forth. Don't fret about the issue of all those things that have been lurking within you. You've been dragging them around for years. You've already survived the worst those particular evil spirits could dish out. Now, lo and behold and bless your soul, you're still standing tall as a man of God. Regardless of the sins the demons manipulated you to imagine or commit, the Lord has never forsaken you. Jesus loves you, and so do I."

With that, Pastor Don reached over to give me another hug. This time there was no bristling from me. I hugged him back and soaked his shirt with joyful tears.

Seeing with New Eyes

Prior to the services that Sunday, I was not accustomed to seeing people lift their hands heavenward in praise. I would have felt awkward to copy them. When I stepped out into the night to walk to my car, however, I raised my hands in thanksgiving to God. I simply felt it appropriate to do so. As I did, I noticed an unusual glistening of the stars and the night's majesty seemed to have a new sheen. It was as though cataracts had been surgically removed from my eyes. Everything around me took on a depth of beauty I had never experienced.

The next morning, an amazed Prudence and I stopped by the church to thank Brother Don. He handed me a dozen or more reel-to-reel tapes. "Jimmy, these are some taped teachings of a minister named Derek Prince. I believe the Lord wants you to get acquainted with his ministry. He's an Englishman with an ability to simplify spiritual truths that is far superior to anyone I've ever heard." Remembering the Birmingham missed connection with Derek, I chuckled at the irony and we headed for home.

On the trip back to Jackson, I was bursting with enthusiasm as I gave Prudence a blow-by-blow description of every aspect of my deliverance session. She cheerfully remarked that I looked and acted more relaxed. Her warm and fuzzy reaction cooled, however, upon hearing of my plans for us to make a return trip to Macon so she could also be set free from any hold evil spirits might have on her life. Even though she had seen firsthand the effect of deliverance from evil spirits and had come to accept its credibility, she doubted that evil spirits could have any substantive effect on her.

We agreed that we would listen to the tapes and see where the Lord led in this wonderful new venture. Remembering the word of prophecy spoken over me in the pastor's office that morning, I could hardly wait.

4

Early Attempts at Deliverance

After our trip to Macon, I consumed Derek Prince's books and tapes with an insatiable appetite. In spite of her initial objections, Prudence was forbearing toward my newfound zeal. My routine evolved into an established pattern: I would listen to a tape and then practice on Prudence.

During one of my practice sessions on her, I rebuked the spirits of awkward shyness and insecurity about her intelligence. We felt sure that they had gained entry from her childhood experiences with an abusive aunt who took care of Prudence and her three siblings during their parents' work hours. More than once the smacks from Aunt Ida's cane—delivered with screams about her stupidity—left welts on Prudence's petite frame. Prudence did not exhibit any noticeable signs of deliverance, but she is a wallflower no more. I have to drag her away from most conversations with visitors at our fellowship, and she is confident and happy about using her many skills.

I began to beat the bushes looking for candidates to whom I could minister. My sales skills came in handy. I had a knack for persuading people to gather groups of their friends to listen to the taped teachings. Afterward, I would offer ministry. As a result, we saw remarkable changes in many lives. I became so diligent to learn all I could from Derek's taped teaching that at times I actually caught myself commanding spirits to leave with a feigned British accent.

Not every one of my early experiences in ministering deliverance was a total success. One time I had invited some college students active with Campus Crusade for Christ to hear a tape. About fifteen students were crammed into the living room of a double-wide house trailer. Toward the end of the tape, one of the young women slipped to the floor and began to flop around. I was petrified, not knowing what to do. I bound the evil spirit and the flopping subsided. Then I asked her to sit in a chair for ministry. Not addressing the evil spirit by any specific or descriptive name, I commanded it to come out of her. To my astonishment, a raspy masculine voice spoke through her lips: "I will not come out."

I decided that the demon might identify itself if ordered to do so. So when I demanded its name, the answer that came was "multiple sclerosis." I quoted some Bible verses that affirmed the authority of believers over demons, and I directed multiple sclerosis to flee from her. The thing gave a mocking laugh and while pointing at the other students said, "If I do, I'll go into her, her and him." The kids scattered like a covey of quail. I found them later, hidden in various rooms of the mobile home.

I addressed the girl by her given name in hopes she would answer in her own voice. She did. I inquired about her condition and learned she was in the early stages of the disease. I apologized for not being able to help her. She wrote down the contact information for Derek Prince Ministries, and I encouraged her to inquire about Derek's itinerary so she could be prayed for by the expert. I went home licking my wounds, my ego pretty badly bruised. Clearly, I had a lot to learn.

A Life-Changing Meeting

As time passed I gained more experience at setting the captives free. This was the 1960s and thousands of kids from the free-love, drug-ridden hippie generation were being swept into the arms of God the Father through the Jesus Movement. The charismatic renewal was in full swing in traditional churches. Many dependable Bible teachers were helping people better understand the biblical legitimacy of the baptism with the Holy Spirit, spiritual gifts and concepts of spiritual warfare.

I had my work cut out for me, between the hippie kids from broken homes and their parents, many of whom had been touched by the Spirit to realize how they had wounded their children. There was no shortage of those seeking deliverance.

I began to support Derek Prince Ministries financially. I was delighted to find his repertoire well-balanced. He had hundreds of teachings apart from the small portion on spiritual warfare themes. We often exchanged letters, and he encouraged me in the progress of my lay ministry.

My first face-to-face encounter with Derek Prince was rather unique. In 1969, I attended a conference where he was speaking. It was held at a Methodist church in downtown Atlanta, Georgia. On the third day, he had two sessions explaining the deliverance ministry.

During the first session, a well-dressed young woman came to the end of the row where I was seated and politely indicated that she would like to pass me in order to take a seat further in. I stood to let her go past me, and, to my shock, when she slipped by I saw a vision of the words *lady of the evening* tattooed across her forehead.

During a break in the teaching, I approached her and said I would like to pose a question to her. She assented, so, hoping to sound tactful, I asked if she had trouble relating to men. Her answer was frank. "Not much. I'm a hooker."

We chatted for a few minutes, and she told me that she had

come for ministry. Later in the meeting, those needing help were all instructed to go to a large room set aside for that purpose. She asked if I would be willing to accompany her, admitting she was afraid to go alone. I consented.

Rather than minister personally to each individual, Derek conducted an *en masse* style of group deliverance. From the podium, he began by calling out various descriptive names of demons, category by category. He began with spirits affecting the emotions such as anxiety, fear and rage. Then he moved on to spirits pertaining to mental fixations like claustrophobia and anorexia. Next, he called out demons that intensify sins of the flesh such as fornication and addiction to pornography. When Derek called out "whoredom," the young woman grabbed my arm and began to thrash about. As I attempted to steady her, I commanded whoredom to leave. She screamed, gagged and began to vomit up large quantities of black, slimy sputum.

Derek saw what was happening and came over to offer assistance. I introduced myself, and explained a little about the situation before him. He recognized my name from our exchange of letters and greeted me warmly. Then he quickly got down to business. He called out numerous other sexual spirits. Many of these made their exit in streams of the blackish mucous. After being set free, the woman regained her composure and raised her hands, laughing and praising the name of the Lord.

From that point on, it was as if Derek and I were joined at the hip. Because my business was seasonal, I was free to join him at his invitation in ministry venues throughout the United States and abroad. In 1974 I entered full-time ministry, and in 1975 I became pastor of the church that sent out Derek and other colleagues of his into ministry. Our friendship and companionship in ministry spanned 35 years until he passed away in 2003. Throughout the years, people would occasionally inquire about how we met. Our standard answer was, "A demon introduced us."

My Wilderness Experience

Before Jesus launched His public ministry, the Holy Spirit led Him into the wilderness. There He underwent forty days of satanic inquisition targeted at raising questions about the legitimacy of His identity and His calling.

My wilderness experience began shortly after meeting Derek and lasted a year. I believe its length and intensity were divinely permitted. In retrospect, the mental assaults served to give me better understanding of the devil's schemes. They certainly gave me greater empathy for those suffering from the enemy's influence.

The New Testament helps us understand that the rain of the Holy Spirit on one's life brings forth good fruit and also exposes troublesome brambles (see Hebrews 6:7–8). I was ecstatic about the sense of well-being and spiritual productivity the anointing of the Spirit fostered in my life. Simultaneously, I was discouraged that His showers of blessing seemed to reveal so many thorns in the soil of my psyche. The attacks on my mind were fierce, wicked, relentless harassment.

First of all, I began to have vile hallucinations that had no justifiable explanation. My family had no history of mental problems, and I had never tampered with recreational drugs. The hallucinations took the form of grotesque assaults on Jesus while He was dying on the cross. The scenes pummeled me day and night. To say I had a hundred daily episodes is not an exaggeration.

Secondly, I was bombarded with insecurities about everything from my salvation to my masculinity. I could easily dismiss the former, but the latter was soul rattling. I did not have effeminate mannerisms. Nor did I have any curiosity or interest in the subject of homosexuality. It was a nonissue until the demons started pounding me.

My efforts to end these unfounded assaults failed completely. I employed every spiritual strategy I knew. Flaming rebukes from the Scriptures did not scorch away the harassment. In desperation, I got rebaptized, but that did not drown out the hallucinations. Fasting did not starve them out.

I made frequent trips to Macon to get help. Pastor VanHoozier's diagnosis was that the assaults were demonic in origin. But those haunting demons were sly. All symptoms of the battle would cease upon my arrival at the church parking lot. They would lie dormant the whole time I was there. The positive side of that dormancy was that the days spent at the church in Macon were more productive. I joined the staff on a part-time basis and matured greatly in my ability to minister to some of those who flocked to the church seeking freedom. On the negative side, as soon as I began my departure back home, the fears and horrific visions would resurface with a vengeance.

After a year of unspeakable torment, I finally got free. I was on my way back to Jackson from Macon and the wicked barrages were pounding me full throttle. I was screaming to the Lord for liberation, even as demonic suggestions of committing suicide ricocheted throughout my mind like bullets from a machine gun.

It was at that critical moment that I heard a little whisper drifting into my consciousness: *Neither life nor death, nor angels, nor powers, nor any created thing can separate you from the love of God in Christ Jesus your Lord.* I recognized those words as a Spirit-inspired rendering of portions of Romans 8:38–39. The effect was immediate.

While driving, I told Satan emphatically that I would not waste another minute with concerns about his antics. He had fired his best shots, but my confidence in God's love for me had never wavered. Furthermore, I affirmed that the Lord knew that my love for Him was unquenchable. As my declaration ended, I sensed relaxation in my spirit, soul and body.

Within a few moments, I had a mental picture of myself playing "cowboy" at the age of four atop my red rocking horse. I was rocking away in pursuit of imaginary villains and "bang-banging" at them with my toy pistol. As I watched, I saw evil spirits entering my abdominal region and settling into compartmentalized nesting places, like pigeons coming home to roost.

I understood this scene to be showing me that the evil spirits tormenting me had entered during my childhood. I commanded the evil spirits of fear and of vile hallucinations to leave me. I felt them depart without any resistance, lifting from my shoulder and streaming out of my ears. From that moment to the present, I have been completely free of that harassment. Not the slightest twinge of those spirits has bothered me again. I can truly testify that "those whom the Son sets free are free indeed."

The invasion by powers of darkness that I saw myself experiencing as a child on the rocking horse were not due to a traumatic home environment. Nor, at that young age, were obvious sins activated in my life. I was just a happy little kid enjoying myself. I cannot offer a definitive reason why they were able to enter me then.

As we noted in chapter 1, there are occasions when either sin or trauma can contribute to the entry of demons, but now I had learned that there does not need to be an instigating factor in every situation. The safe ground, again, is to recognize that evil spirits are opportunists, and treat them as such. In their craving to enter human vessels, they can and do enter innocent victims through whom they attempt to express their satanically assigned purposes.

The tactics of demons function like those of pedophiles: All they need is for the victim to be alone and oblivious to the danger. We will explore pertinent factors in both the "cause and effect" models and the "no-fault" models of demonic invasion in upcoming chapters.

But, What If?

Regularly during periods of personal worship, I ponder "what if" questions: What if I had never heard about and received deliverance? Is it possible that the spirits compelling me to fantasize about women and to masturbate could have seduced me into becoming an adulterer? Might I have grown so tired of suppressing my inner anger that I would have become a tyrant and destroyed our family life? Is there any way under heaven I could have spiraled into insanity and degradation as a result of the hallucinations?

All of those things have happened to conscientious husbands

and Christian statesmen no less committed to righteousness than I. Biblical knowledge and real-life experience confirm that the types of demons that plagued my life, as well as multitudes of other types, are common and widespread. They are as active in affluent Christianized Western democracies as they are in tribal communities of Third World nations.

The Word of God tells us in Hosea 4:6 that God's people are destroyed due to lack of knowledge. The familiar adage "What you don't know can't hurt you" is a lie. What we don't know has infinite capacity to hurt us and those whom we hold dear.

In the next chapter we will expand our knowledge of demonic intentions to degrade and destroy human beings. There is war in the heavens of which we should be aware.

5

Learning about Satan's Kingdom

*There are two equal and opposite errors into which our race can
fall about the devils. One is to disbelieve in their existence. The
other is to believe, and to feel an excessive and unhealthy interest
in them. They themselves are equally pleased with both errors and
hail a materialist or a magician with the same delight.*

—C. S. LEWIS, *THE SCREWTAPE LETTERS*

Skeptics consider the idea of invisible evil powers to be primitive
foolishness and religious nonsense. Proponents counter that Satan,
his angels and evil spirits surely influence our day-to-day lives. The
only point the two sides might agree on is the universal claim of
their existence.

Along with the Jewish Tanakh and Christian Bible, the mytholo-
gies, literature and art of multiple religions and civilizations have,
for centuries, featured evil spiritual entities dwelling in a parallel
dimension with access to human populations.

The descriptions of these creatures vary widely. The king of evil,
Satan, is usually portrayed as a malicious-looking giant with wings
and horns. Evil angels reflect his image, but are normally smaller.

Some have wings; others do not. Demons are often depicted as ugly monkey-like entities that are diminutive in stature. Many are red in color with reptilian scales, and others have ghoulishly pale skin.

A number of nations lay claim to spirit beings with humanlike features and behavior that ranges from mischievous benevolence to orneriness to evil destruction. In the British Isles, Europe and Scandinavia, it is the fairies, leprechauns, elves, dwarves, goblins, hobgoblins and trolls. Islam has its *jinns*. The water spirits of West Africa and the *duwendes* of the Philippines also have human features.

Two Examples of Sightings

Do these physical descriptions sound farfetched? Undoubtedly so! Yet, while it is not a day-to-day occurrence for most of us, sightings of evil spiritual creatures are actually not so unusual. Here are two stories that show what I mean.

A couple of years ago in the late fall, I was hunting wild boar in a Florida wildlife area with two of my grandsons. Tino was eleven years old and Michael was nine at the time. The boys were outpacing me, with Tino in the lead.

Suddenly, he yelled, "Rattlesnake!" I rushed to his side and found him standing still, paralyzed with fright. A two-foot snake was rattling and strike-coiled within three feet of the boy. I shot it, and when I was sure Tino wanted to continue with our hunting trip, we walked on.

I settled the boys on hunting stands and took a place between them. About fifteen minutes had passed when Tino walked to my side. He was visibly shaken, and his lips quivered as he spoke.

"Baba, I saw a red monkey-looking thing sitting on a branch. It had its arms folded and was staring at me like it was really mad."

I explained that it was probably the demon that had caused the rattlesnake to cross his path. "The devil wanted to hurt us by one of us getting snake-bitten. One of the Lord's angels kept it from biting you so I could get into position to shoot it."

I thanked God for saving Tino, and commanded all demonic powers to leave the vicinity.

I instructed my grandson about what to do if the evil spirit appeared again. "Tell it you are protected by the angels of God and the blood of Jesus and that you're not afraid of it. Then order it to go away in the name of Jesus." Reassured, Tino returned to his place and there were no more appearances.

I believe Tino's sighting was authentic. His family attends a Presbyterian church that does not provide teaching about satanic matters. Prudence and I, when the grandchildren visit, do not make a habit of focusing on the topic of demons. There is no reason to assume Tino was predisposed to imagine a demon sighting.

Another example occurred several years ago when I was invited to speak at a church in General Santos City on Mindanao Island of the Philippines. I was accompanied by a young man named Ralph, a promising evangelist.

Whenever venturing into unfamiliar ministry locales, it is my custom to arrive several days early. I spend the time there studying the nation's political and religious histories and observing the culture. My objective is to better understand the population's perspectives. Having done that, I can intercede for them more intelligently and have greater chances to minister effectively to their needs. On this trip, my studies led me to understand that Filipinos frequently have interactions with spirit beings.

The most commonly reported encounters are with mystical creatures called *duwendes*. They are something like elves. *Duwendes* dwell in trees, caves and earthen mounds. They are said to come out mostly at night, but also at noon each day. These imps are reputed to bring good fortune if acknowledged, but are believed to be capable of imposing curses if ignored. It is not unusual for Filipinos to leave offerings of food around areas suspected to be their lairs. Children often speak of a playful *duwende* joining in their games.

While preparing for the first service, I heard a local radio newsman comment on finding the tracks of a *duwende* in the dust on his office desk. Several hours later, Pastor Burt, pastor of the church where I would be speaking, phoned and asked for help in ministering to the daughter of one of his parishioners. She had been hospitalized in a catatonic state. I dispatched my evangelist associate, Ralph, to handle the assignment.

Ralph accompanied Pastor Burt to the young lady's room. Her bed was encircled by her parents and about four members of the hospital's staff. The lead physician said he was mystified by her condition, as he could find no medical reasons for it. Ralph placed his hands upon the still figure, praying for her to be revived.

He then remembered my mention of the *duwende* phenomenon and decided to insert a rebuke of those entities into his prayer. She snapped to consciousness. The young lady told the assembled group that she had seen a *duwende* that morning, and it frightened her so badly she had passed out. The medical team was deeply impressed by her speedy recovery.

Ralph presented the plan of salvation, and all of the staff members present confessed Jesus as Savior and Lord. At the service that evening, the parents testified of their daughter's deliverance, and there was successful ministry to others as a result.

The Structure of Satan's Kingdom

Most Bible students recognize the existence of an evil entity called Satan, who presides over a kingdom. Prior to becoming God's enemy, the devil served God as the archangel Lucifer, an anointed cherub.

At some point in past ages, Lucifer grew tired of subservience to God and instigated an insurrection, persuading a third of the angels to join him in trying to overthrow God's Kingdom. (See Isaiah 14:12–15; Ezekiel 28:11–17; Revelation 12:2–4, 7–9.) The rebellion failed, Lucifer was renamed Satan, the adversary, and he was ejected from God's presence along with the other insurrectionist angels, generally referred to as fallen angels.

Subsequent to his defeat, Satan established a kingdom composed of these fallen angels and other types of evil spirits. His kingdom is located in the heavenly realms, and its influence extends throughout the earth.

Military Order

The New Testament provides a sketch of Satan's domain. It is structured much like a military hierarchy. The devil is commander-in-chief; the fallen angels are his officers; demons are the trench soldiers. Although arguably open to interpretation, numerous details in the Bible relate to the structure and activity of Satan's kingdom. (My assessment follows. For further biblical study regarding the structure of this kingdom, please refer to the various teachings of Derek Prince and Don Basham, particularly Derek's book, *War in Heaven* [Chosen, 2003] and Don's book, *Deliver Us from Evil* [Chosen, 2005].)

Regarding Satan's rulership, the Bible tells us that he is the father of lies; the god of this age; the prince of the power of the air; and Beelzebub, the ruler of demons (see Matthew 12:24; John 8:44; 2 Corinthians 4:4). The combined titles indicate authoritative rule from heavenly regions extending into the earth below. From the heavenlies, Satan's forces wage ongoing war against the purposes of God and anything that would ultimately benefit mankind.

Two passages from Paul's epistle to the Ephesians (2:1–4 and 6:11–12) reveal that we are not battling flesh and blood: Christians are wrestling with principalities, powers and the rulers of darkness in heavenly places. People who are unconverted or disobedient to God are particularly vulnerable to being manipulated and controlled by these spirits.

Locations under Siege

Since the Bible talks about the heavenly *places*, we understand that there is more than one. In 2 Corinthians 12:1–2, Paul spoke of being ushered into the presence of God in the third heaven. As Derek Prince often said in his teachings on the subject, logic would lead us to believe that if there is a third heaven, there is also a first and a second.

The third heaven, the dwelling place of God, is in the uttermost territories of the universe. The second heaven is in the upper atmosphere of the planet. The first heaven is the oxygen-filled atmosphere surrounding us. Satan's kingdom is located in those lower two heavens.

The functional structure over which the devil reigns in the two heavens is principalities. A *principality* is a territory with defined borders under the rule of a government. In the second heaven, the devil's headquarters sit, like the tip of a pyramid, over a broader expanse occupied by high-ranking fallen angels. They have the ability to travel into the lowest, first, heaven, commanding the demons that reside on earth.

Fallen angels and demons can project disruptive thoughts into humankind. The more common type of attack comes from demons. Demons wage war on two fronts. One front is our atmosphere, with its close proximity to humans; they can whisper from perches on shoulders quite effectively. The other front is actually within the physical bodies of some humans. Many demonic spirits crave human bodies as the means to act out their particular type of evil activity.

War in the Heavenlies

On a level high above us, God's angels from the third heaven and Satan's fallen angels in the second heaven are regularly engaged in battle. One of those engagements is spoken of in Daniel 10. An angelic messenger was sent from God's presence to Daniel in response to the prophet's prayer and fasting. The messenger told Daniel that he would have arrived earlier were it not for the opposition of the prince of Persia, a fallen angel. He described how the archangel Michael had helped him break through. The implication is that the skirmish took place somewhere in the principality over Persia.

The messenger further disclosed (see verses 20–21) that he anticipated another collision in the second heaven with the prince of Persia upon his return to God's dwelling place. The angel also prophesied that the prince of Persia would be replaced by the prince of Greece in the future. That apparently happened when Alexander the Great conquered the Persian Empire.

The episode in Daniel suggests to us that events on earth are paralleled by events taking place between the powers of light and darkness in the heavens. The battleground is in the second heaven, intermediate between the throne of God and the earth.

God's people participate in the skirmishes in two ways. First, our prayers strengthen the holy angels to wage war successfully. Second, believers can also seriously weaken Satan's grip by expelling demonic trench soldiers from the souls and bodies of humans throughout the world.

Where Did Demons Originate?

As we have noted thus far, it is my understanding from Scripture that Satan's commanders are, like him, fallen angels. Demons, I believe, are evil spirits of a lower species subservient to Satan and his fallen angels.

The Bible does not offer a detailed account of the origin of demonic spirits, and the area remains too much of a theological mystery to cling dogmatically to any one stance. While it is helpful to have some idea about what demons are and where they come from, ultimately the issue is not the origin of demons. The more crucial matter in this area is clear understanding that evil spirits exist, along with knowledge of how to deal with them.

Still, it is good to have acquaintance with the various theories about the origin of demonic spirits. One view is that demons are fallen angels, ousted from access to God for participating in Satan's rebellion. A second view regards demons as the disembodied spirits of human-like beings that possibly inhabited the earth prior to the six days of Creation. A third view is similar. It is the belief of a few that demons are the disembodied spirits of the offspring of fallen angels and human women that perished in the flood of Noah's day (see Genesis 6:1–7, 17). A fourth view comes from Jewish folklore. It suggests that demons are the disembodied spirits of dead humans whose sinful souls have not found rest.

None of the aforementioned explanations fit within my comfort zones. Over the years as I have pondered the possible origin of demons, a view has evolved in my thinking that seems scripturally tenable. It answers the question of why God permits demons to exist. I offer it for your consideration, but I do not regard it as a set-in-stone matter. I believe demons are a category of spirit beings inferior to angels, created by God during the period in which He created Lucifer and the other angels.

Why Demons Exist

Let's begin with the fact that God is the supreme ruler and creator of all things. At some point in eternity past, the divine council of the Godhead in the Trinity decided to extend the family of God. God said, "Let us make man in our image." In the harmony of the Trinity, man was created to govern the earth. Creation in God's image included the freedom for mankind to make decisions in accordance with his own desires. Inherent with man's free will were options for rebellion against God's will as well as compliance with it.

In keeping with God's goodness and mercy, His desire was for good to befall mankind. However, in keeping with God's justice and severity, there had to be detrimental consequences if man's free will chose rebellion (see Romans 11:22). The Lord inserted mechanisms into the scaffolding of creation that would trigger innumerable penalties in the event that Adam and Eve chose rebellious paths. Beyond God's setting the mechanism into place, there was no necessity for God to be the on-site administrator of the punitive consequences that would trouble mankind. With rare exceptions, the consequential punishments functioned like an automatic sowing-and-reaping chain reaction. Of course, we know that God is intimately involved with us as His cherished creation. He is not an "absentee landlord." But He has clearly designed much about life and creation to progress in a spontaneous way, including the punishments mentioned above.

Adam and Eve ignored God's warning that the sin of eating the forbidden fruit would bring death. The couple had no concept about the extensive penalties that the power of sin and death would bring upon them and their descendants. As a result of their disobedience, the consequences were activated.

Colossians 1:16 speaks of the Lord creating visible and invisible things in the heavens and on the earth. Unbeknownst to Adam and Eve, there was an invisible dimension in immediate proximity to the visible beauty and function of the Garden of Eden. The invisible realm surrounding them contained all of the wickedness under Satan's domain. It consisted of the powers of sin, death, fallen angels and demons.

Aside from Satan's sneak attack in temptation while disguised as a serpent, the powers of sin, death, fallen angels and demons were kept in check by man's obedience to God. It is possible that prior to the Fall, demons were confined to a prison called the bottomless pit, the abyss.

During Jesus' ministry, demons exemplified familiarity with the abyss and begged Him not to send them there before the appointed time. The book of Revelation speaks about how in the end times two new varieties of spirit beings will be loosed from the abyss upon rebellious people. *Dake's Annotated Reference Bible* defines them as demons. They will be fierce in appearance. One type will be shaped like horses and will have wings; faces like men; teeth like lions; long hair like women; and tails with stingers like scorpions. The second type will be demonic horses ridden by an army of two hundred million. The demon horses will have heads like lions and poisonous serpents for tails rather than hair. They will wipe out one-third of the earth's population through the fire, smoke and brimstone that bellows from their mouths and from the bites of the snake heads at the tips of their tails (see Genesis 2:10–14; Matthew 8:29; Luke 8:31; Revelation 9).

Adam and Eve's disobedience in eating of the forbidden fruit was the mechanism that triggered the unleashing of the punitive consequences into life on earth. Man's invisible enemies of Satan, fallen angels and demons were loosed to intensify the heartaches of sin and death.

After the Fall of man, Satan, his cohort angels and the spiritual beings called demons afflicted every dynamic of human affairs. Interpersonal relationships were made subject to corruption. Fear and insecurity became commonplace. Immune systems were weakened, opening the door for disease, tumors, viral germs and infectious bacteria. Addictions to derivatives of plants were injected into the equation. Demons can have roles in any of these afflictions. Some taunt and tempt from without. Others succeed in infesting aspects of human personality and physical bodies. The solution for all sufferers is to call upon the name of Jesus for deliverance.

The Nature of Demons

Demons seem to exhibit some manner of human attributes. Jesus' mention of their ability to wander, presumably to walk, implies the possession of some type of appendage allowing mobility. Modern and biblical reports tell us that they are occasionally visible to the naked eye. They are known to move inanimate objects. Such things suggest that evil spirits can exhibit material qualities even though they are spirit beings.

The encounters Jesus had with demons indicate that they have human-like psychological characteristics—individual personalities. There are six basic components that signify personhood: volition, intellect, emotion, memory, imagination and the ability to communicate. The following two Bible passages demonstrate that demons possess those features:

[Jesus said,] "When an unclean spirit goes out of a man, he goes through dry places, seeking rest; and finding none, he says, 'I will return to my house from which I came.' And when he comes, he finds it swept and put in order. Then he goes and takes with him seven other spirits more wicked than himself, and they enter and dwell there; and the last state of that man is worse than the first."

LUKE 11:24–26

You believe that there is one God. You do well. Even the demons believe—and tremble!

JAMES 2:19

For an evil spirit to decide to return to his former habitation requires volition to make the decision and memory to recall its host's identity and location. The evicted spirit's reentry with seven more wicked spirits implies that it has communicated with them. The fact that demons tremble about the existence of God points to the possession of emotions, intellect and imagination. Intellect is needed to evaluate decisions to believe or to disbelieve. As it is with humans, so it is with demons: It takes imagination to activate emotional trembling.

The Dominion Mandate

The first couple's decision to disobey God in the Garden signaled that they were relinquishing governorship of the world to Satan's authority. In a manner of speaking, they renounced membership in the family of God. The born-again experience opens the way for our adoption back into His family. It also empowers those who belong to Jesus to know victory in the war with these unseen enemies. We have the opportunity to rectify the actions of Adam and Eve that opened the gate for evil to come in. As of now, the rectification is not complete. But great inroads will be made before the Lord's appearing.

On the sixth day of Creation, God's earthly family was commissioned to export the order and tranquil beauty of the Garden of Eden to the untamed corners of the world (see Genesis 1:26–28). That commission is often referred to as the "dominion mandate," and the Lord has never withdrawn it. His command to the Body of Christ, those adopted back into His family, is to rectify the wrongs perpetrated by our first ancestors. Our redemption through the atoning death and resurrection of Christ empowers us to expel evil spirits from working their torment in our own lives and from the lives of those coming to us for help.

This concept, of course, assumes that Christians are truly in a battle with demons, and that they sometimes find themselves wounded by these invisible enemies. This brings us to the often misguided topic of "possession" by the enemy and his hordes. How far can the enemy go in molesting the lives of believers? What about unbelievers? Let's study Scripture for a clear understanding of the lines of battle that the enemy can—and cannot—cross.

6

The Christian Dilemma

Deliverance is not an uncomplicated topic. It is no surprise, therefore, that Christians ponder it with some confusion and conflict. First, many born-again individuals seem to come to the Lord relatively demon-free. Second, some people who were troubled by evil spirits seem to have been freed from them the moment they confessed Jesus as Lord. For some reason in their lives (yet not in others), the powers of darkness could not endure the light of Christ and fled the scene.

Those two camps have difficulty identifying with the plight of a third category of Christians. This category consists of those who came to the Lord with demonic issues and remain in that state. It is also possible, as we will see in a moment, for Christians to make unwise decisions following their conversions and open the door for these invisible enemies.

Believers who have never experienced demonic problems are often at odds with Christians who complain about demonic attacks. They mistakenly interpret the harassment described by their "less fortunate brethren" as simply evidence of mankind's fallen and undisciplined nature. With best intentions, they tell them to get a grip and get right with God.

The "afflicted" believers on the other side, however, find it impossible to make lasting changes on their own. Consequently, committed Christians who are dealing with evil spirits are left to flounder.

That was my exact situation. In dealing with this perplexing issue, let me relate my testimony of what I have experienced as a circumspect servant of the Lord.

Early Background

I was raised in a devout, conservative evangelical home. My birth was two months premature. Christian friends throughout the United States were praying for my survival. I was put into an incubator and kept there for three months. In those days physical contact beyond feeding, diaper changes and medications for babies in incubators was not encouraged.

To add to this situation, my father was a military officer. During the turmoil surrounding my birth, he was assigned to a battalion in another state. Since my mother could not give me the physical contact she hoped to provide, nor could she care for me directly as she longed to do, she moved out-of-state with my father. At this time, gas was being rationed, and their visits to me were few and far between prior to my discharge. As a sickly infant, I was left alone, my father and mother far from the hospital where I was receiving care. Opportunities to experience familial affections were practically nonexistent.

At the age of five, I turned into quite a preacher. I would admonish anyone who would listen about the waiting dangers of hell's fire and would entreat them to repent and to get saved. The novelty of a dynamo tike-preacher was a family trophy. I was often called upon to entertain my parents' guests.

When I was eight, my eager-to-please disposition turned in the opposite direction. I grew stubborn and began to resist just about anything my mother or father asked me to do. The older I got, the stronger the resistance became. Even though I was usually sorry afterward, my rebellious episodes looked like harbingers of parent hatred.

When I was nine, Mom and Dad encouraged me to "walk the aisle" in our Baptist church to confess Christ publicly and to be immersed in the waters of baptism. Even though I was already born again, I think my parents had two hopes for the aisle trip: that it would fulfill an expected rite of passage for Christian youngsters (my younger sister would take her turn a few years later), and that it would rectify my behavioral problems, or so they prayed.

An Ominous Forecast

Despite my public profession of Christ and baptism, little changed. Hardly a week would pass when I did not have a flare-up catapulting the entire household into confusion and frustration. Afterward, I was always sorrowful and would pray and read my Bible in contrition. It did not help. My mysterious behavior was about to take a dreadful twist.

When we were living in Newport, Rhode Island, I was twelve and in the sixth grade. I hurt my elbow in a bike crash. While wincing with pain, I heard these words coming from my lips as I shook my fist heavenward: "God, I hate You. Get out of my life, and leave me alone forever." I note with thanks and to the glory of His name that He ignored that prayer and never abandoned me.

When I was 24 I had a supernatural encounter with the Spirit of God in a motel room. I became an intensely spiritual-minded Christian and a soul winner. But to my shock, my agitation against my mother and father did not diminish. All of us—my parents, my wife and I—sensed there was something very wrong with me. Our observations were correct, but we simply did not have a broad enough biblical perspective to make an accurate diagnosis. Like the majority of Christians, for us the concept that a believer could have demonic issues was completely off the screen of our spiritual radar. How quickly we were to find out one simple fact: We were wrong.

Within less than two years of the Lord touching me in the motel room, I was introduced to the ministry of Derek Prince. I was liberated from numerous spirits. I assumed I had also been set free from my problem of hating my parents, although nothing specific took place to effect that freedom.

For the next 29 years I was further encouraged as the episodes of frustration with my parents seemed to fall within normal ranges for an adult child toward parental authority. I did not know that the rage was lying dormant. Then in 1995, an event took place that initiated the process of truly getting free.

That year, I was in a minor car accident. The air bags in my car, which should have deployed normally as the result of a fender bender, instead, exploded. At that moment, tiny particles from the ruptured air bags went directly into my eyes. As a result of that explosion, I was rendered legally blind.

Within about two years of that accident, to my dismay and that of my parents, my intolerance of them resurfaced with a vengeance. Even though I loved them deeply, our interaction was as explosive as those air bags. During that time, if my mom or dad tried to speak into any issue of my life, I erupted in absolute fury.

Most of our family visits during those days ended abruptly after a couple of hours. At most, visits with them would last a day before the fury broke out. The irony of my situation was that by this time I had ministered deliverance to thousands of people on four continents, yet I did not have a clue that my problem was demonic in nature. I thought it stemmed solely from my parents' unwelcome habit of sticking their noses into my affairs. To my shame, my animosity even continued in me following their deaths. Frequently, at hearing favorable memories of them, I would feel compelled to refute what was being said with negative tidbits of gossip and unflattering remarks.

At the age of 66, I sought the Lord earnestly about this matter of my rotten attitude toward my parents. As I prayed I saw, in my mind's eye, Jesus taking me back to my months in the incubator as an infant. I began to sense how I had felt at that time. Revelatory insights came instantly. The lack of familial attention and affection had made me feel abandoned and irrelevant. The repeated pounding of those painful emotions had wounded my soul, allowing the entrance into my life of a demon of hatred toward my parents.

Once I recognized that truth, I asked the Lord to deliver me and to give me His peace. He did so through a symbolic vision. I saw Jesus blessing children. He reached over a number of the children surrounding Him to pick up a tiny infant to embrace. As He smiled down at the baby, I recognized its face as my own. With that revelation, the presence of God flooded every fabric of my being. And at that moment, the demon that had sparked my rebellious animosity toward my mother and father left me. Today, any mention of my dad and mom evokes within me expressions of fond appreciation and love for them.

I cannot explain why, following the car accident, those disdainful emotions resurged in me after so many years of dormancy. It is a mystery, as are many facets of the deliverance ministry. Dealing with the demonic realm is similar to the mystery of male/female relationships in that it is not an exact science.

There may be one of two explanations for those calmer years. Possibly, I was inhabited by two closely related spirits. (At times, evil spirits can affect a person in a cluster.) All I can surmise is that one demon left when I first received deliverance ministry. The other did not. The other explanation could be that there was only one spirit of parental rebellion that slyly chose to lie dormant for all those years. I lean toward the latter view.

What I have shared so far in this chapter punctuates three realities. First, the devil plots his schemes years in advance in people's lives, only to have them erupt strategically at the most inopportune time. Second, demons do not play fair, and Christians are as susceptible to their treachery and influence as anyone else. Third, the good news is, of course, that freedom is available in Jesus' name.

Biblical Protocol

One common denominator for Christians who have demonic issues is that deliverance was not ministered to them at salvation. In fact, they were not evangelized in keeping with biblical protocols. I am not aware of one single traditional Christian denomination that practices authentic, full-blown New Testament evangelism.

Jesus and His disciples set the pattern for evangelism. The certifying signs identifying them as representatives of the Kingdom of God were healing the sick and expelling demons (see Matthew 12:28; Luke 11:20). The example they set was duplicated by Philip the Evangelist and the apostolic ministries of the early Church.

Philip was the only Bible character specifically labeled with the title of evangelist. His ministry brought people to faith in Jesus' divinity and Lordship. He did not consider his efforts for new converts complete unless they had been baptized in water and in the Holy Spirit. But that was not all: He further emphasized healing the sick and expelling demons (see Acts 8:5–8, 12, 14–17).

Most contemporary people come into the spiritual dimensions of Philip's ministry more or less on "the installment plan." The first installment is saving grace; the second, water baptism; the third, the infilling of the Holy Spirit. To the glory of God, considerable numbers eventually discover resources of teaching about faith for physical healing. Relatively few, however, are ever informed that deliverance from evil spirits is as applicable today as it was in the first century.

Similar to what I experienced, even after years of devoted service to Christ, too many godly people are left adrift to struggle with demonically inspired aspects of sin, inner conflict and relational dysfunction.

Dispelling an Incorrect Premise

Those who oppose the idea that a believer might be troubled by demons often lean on an error-ridden cliché: "God will not dwell in or use an unclean vessel." This concept is easily dismissed by the teaching of the Bible. The apostle Paul, for instance, thanked God for the members of the church at Corinth, and commended them for not failing to exercise all of the spiritual gifts that bear witness to the indwelling Holy Spirit. In the same epistle, he rebuked the Corinthians for their widespread immorality (see 1 Corinthians 1:4–7; 5:1).

At least four other Bible passages either hint at or proclaim that Christians can host evil spirits. First, the New Testament speaks of nine gifts of the Holy Spirit that are meant to be used for Christian assemblies and for evangelism (see 1 Corinthians 12:7–11). One of the gifts, the discerning of spirits, enables Christians to distinguish one type of spirit from another type of spirit.

Discernment uncovers that which is not obvious. There is not much point in applying the gift of the distinguishing of spirits toward unbelievers who might attend a church function, for it would be evident that Christ's Spirit does not dwell within them. It is within the context of believers ministering to believers where discernment becomes a necessity (see 1 John 4:1–4).

Second, Paul warned his constituents that it is possible for Christians to receive a different spirit from the Holy Spirit who took up residence within them at salvation (see 2 Corinthians 11:3–4). The passage contains the phrase "if you receive a different spirit." The word for *receive* is the same word used for receiving the Holy Spirit, which is an inner reception. The Greek word for *different* denotes "another spirit of a different sort." If a spirit differs in sort from the Holy Spirit, it has to be an unholy spirit, essentially a demon.

The third passage indicates that Christians can become infested by evil spirits after their conversions. Revelation 18:1–4 urges God's people to come out of Babylon lest they receive her plagues. Those plagued will become the dwelling places for demons. The passage conveys the understanding that Babylon is the worldly system that encourages immorality. We all know of Christians who are living examples of having one foot in the Kingdom of God and the other in the kingdom of darkness. They do so at great risk of becoming the habitations of evil spirits.

The fourth passage that refers to evil spirit activities within Christians is James 3:8–13. Through symbolism, the verses give a subtle hint about demonic infestations. The apostle questioned how his constituents were able to bless the brethren in church and later curse them at home. He wanted to know how the single faucet of the human mouth could bring forth two contrasting types of water, fresh and bitter. With tremendous understatement, James feigned confusion about the matter.

Actually, James was very well aware that Jesus had said that the Holy Spirit within believers would be like a spring gushing forth rivers of living water from the mouth of a Christian (see John 7:37–39). James's innuendo was that one mouth (faucet) bringing forth both freshwater and saltwater indicated the presence of two springs rather than just one. One spring was the Holy Spirit, and the other spring an unholy spirit.

The fact that God dwells in and uses unclean vessels is evident. Far too often we hear news broadcasts about champions of the faith, people who have had genuine conversion experiences, being caught in scurrilous sins. After being exposed, most speak of incessant attempts to shake free from their temptations, with continual prayers of repentance and vows to sin no more. When citing reasons for the persistent failures, a common thread appears in the responses of many: "I felt helpless. There was something in me that drove me to sin."

That describes precisely the activities of demons.

Confusing Terminology

There is a term used in numerous Bible translations that leads Christians to think that deliverance could not be applicable to them. The term is *demon-possessed*. The word *possessed* is the stumbling block. It implies ownership by demons, suggesting that a person is under their complete control. Believers reason that *possession* could not be possible because they have voluntarily submitted the ownership of their lives to Christ and are able to function normally in most aspects.

The use of the word *demon-possessed* is an unfortunate translation. It presents a skewed perception about the actual condition of most of the people to whom Jesus ministered deliverance. The majority of people brought to Jesus had the ability to function normally. With most, demonic activities were restricted to isolated aspects of their lives. The madman who lived in tombs and the mute boy who had seizures were exceptions.

The word *demon-possessed* is a translation of the Greek word *daimonizomai*. *Strong's Hebrew and Greek Dictionary* defines this as "to be exercised by a demon or to have a demon." That rendering of *daimonizomai* is used in this example from the gospel of John: "Others said, 'These are not the words of one who *has a demon*. Can a demon open the eyes of the blind?'" (John 10:21, emphasis added).

"Demon possession" is a misleading, inaccurate translation. A definition of *daimonizomai* that is more in keeping with the biblical meaning is "under the influence of an evil spirit in a specific area of one's health, emotions or personality."

Forget Hollywood

If you have based your concept of Christians being afflicted by demons on the dramatizations of the entertainment industry, be assured it does not depict New Testament deliverance with even the slightest note of authenticity. Most commercial depictions emphasize ancient rituals of exorcism that have little in common with the biblical methods. When we know our authority in Christ, deliverance holds no dangers for us or for the people we help.

Do people occasionally convulse, wrench, cough or vomit? Yes! Do demons ever speak from people's lips during deliverance sessions? Yes! Such happenings, however, are rare. And when they do occur, they are like snapshots taken at spontaneous, temporarily embarrassing moments. No one would interpret them as being representative of a person's entire life and demeanor.

Consider this thought. Prior to deliverance, demons regularly drive their hosts to commit undignified acts. Arguments ensue over nonsense. Eyes bulge and blood vessels swell under the heat of out-of-control emotions. Husbands put their fists through walls and later have to face the quizzical expressions of visitors to their homes. Wives and mothers throw tantrums in front of the kids, and let loose with shrill screams within earshot of the neighbors. Demon-inspired actions can cause people years of embarrassment. In comparison, any antics an evil spirit might display when commanded to exit are momentary.

It is highly unlikely that you would have acute verbal or physical manifestations during deliverance. If it begins to happen, the strength of your human spirit can enable you to regain control so the session can continue. If you happen to spit out something, the novelty will soon pass. The truth is you have eliminated far more and far worse in the course of a bout with the flu!

Most deliverance sessions are quite mild. Just as most people do not feel demons enter, most people do not feel them leave. The proof of effectual deliverance is not the occurrence of bizarre exits. The proof is measurable changes for the better from whatever maladies of soul the demons were causing.

Deliverance is a wonderful tool the Lord has provided for each of us through His death and miraculous resurrection. There is really no sensible reason not to evaluate whether or not we need liberation, and then pursue it in obedience to the Lord. In the next chapter, we will explore Jesus' teaching about exorcism, and the most usual gateways to infiltration by demons.

Jesus and the Exorcists

Every time I read through the gospels, I am impressed by the number of people who came to Jesus seeking deliverance from evil spirits. The operative word that captivates me is *many*. The Scriptures speak about "many" coming to Jesus for deliverance, the casting out of "many" demons and demons coming out of "many" (see Matthew 8:16; Mark 6:13; Luke 4:41).

Jesus cast out demons from people in synagogues and His open-air meetings, as well as while conversing one-on-one. Jesus ministered deliverance to people from every strata of society: working-class people, women of means, children and a madman who lived in tombs. Clearly, Jesus dealt with "many" demons in "many" people in "many" locales. No matter what the venue, deliverance was a dominant theme of His life's work.

In addition, the Messiah chose His twelve disciples and commanded them to go throughout the cities of Israel casting out demons and healing the sick. Later, He gave the same command to seventy more workers. That adds up to 82 people, or 41 two-person teams, being activated to liberate the oppressed.

At that time, there were no more than a hundred cities and villages in Israel. We can make an educated "guesstimate" that, once commissioned, Jesus' 41 teams kept their hands to the plow and ministered for a minimum of two consecutive years. The limited number of villages, the large number of teams and the length of the ministry years suggests that each team made more than one visit to each city.

Adding that up, the implications are that many, many people needed deliverance.

It is interesting to note that when the seventy returned to report their success, the aspect of ministry that thrilled them most was dominion over demons. The Lord shifted the focus, encouraging them to keep the joy of eternal life uppermost in their thinking. Nonetheless, the Scriptures convey that at that very moment the Lord was filled with joy because the seventy had grasped the concept of authority over satanic powers (see Luke 10:1, 17–21).

Ancient Jewish Exorcists

In relation to demonic issues, the people of ancient Israel had a distinct advantage over most people of our day. For the Jews of old, concerns about demonic invasions in their lives were no more unusual than concerns about airborne germs are for us. Just as we are not embarrassed to shop for a reputable doctor, they did not consider it humiliating to ask about the name of an effective exorcist. It was customary to seek out whichever source of help—physician or exorcist—the circumstances might dictate.

In the societies of that Mediterranean world, Jewish people were well known for producing skilled exorcists. The exorcists had a ritualistic approach and used a variety of incantations, potions and amulets with their clients. (An amulet is generally an ornament of folk jewelry worn to ward off evil and ensure good fortune for clients of occultists.)

Respected Jewish historian Flavius Josephus spoke of Solomon, son of King David, composing incantations for driving away demons. In his book *Antiquities of the Jews*, Josephus gives his eyewitness account of an exorcism using King Solomon's incantations and techniques and suggests that Solomon's name was an effective tool. This exorcism took place among the troops under the command of the Roman Emperor Vespasian. The officiating exorcist was named Eleazar.

> [F]or I have seen a certain man of my own country, whose name was Eleazar, releasing people that were demoniacal in the presence of Vespasian, and his sons, and his captains, and the whole multitude of his soldiers. The manner of the cure was this: He put a ring that had a root of one of those sorts mentioned by Solomon to the nostrils of the demoniac, after which he drew out the demon through his nostrils; and when the man fell down immediately, he abjured him to return into him no more, making still mention of Solomon, and reciting the incantations which he composed. And when Eleazar would persuade and demonstrate to the spectators that he had such a power, he set a little way off a cup or basin full of water, and commanded the demon, as he went out of the man, to overturn it, and thereby to let the spectators know that he had left the man; and when this was done, the skill and wisdom of Solomon was shown very manifestly.*

> *FLAVIUS JOSEPHUS, *ANTIQUITIES OF THE JEWS*, TRANS. WILLIAM WHISTON (PUBLIC DOMAIN, 1737), 574–576.

Today we might consider this story to be nothing but the showmanship of charlatans. Jesus apparently did not hold that perspective. In Luke 11:15–26, quoting one of His exchanges with the Pharisees, we read His comments on exorcists. When the Pharisees accused Jesus of using satanic powers to cast out demons, He asked how their sons were able to cast out unclean spirits. Jesus' rebuttal acknowledged that the exorcists did have a measure of effectiveness.

Jesus remarked further about the ultimate results for those ministered to by these exorcists. The implications of His comments are somewhat veiled for us, but were clear to His audience. He seemed to be hinting at the short-lived results of their methods: Even though exorcists routinely conjured demons out, they had no way of keeping them out. After a temporary period, an ousted spirit often reentered his host. When a demon did so, it might take along seven other spirits more malicious than itself. The person's final condition was worse than it was before getting an exorcism. Not so with the ministries of Jesus and His disciples.

Jesus' Deliverance Ministry

When the ministry of Jesus came on the scene, the Jews of Israel witnessed a dramatic shift in all they had known about deliverance. Jesus did not conjure out spirits with ritualistic incantations. He did not need to borrow Solomon's name and authority. There was no need for His disciples to haul around inventories of anti-demon trinkets and protective household items.

Jesus expelled demons from people's bodies and personalities simply by commanding them to go. He was the Word of God incarnate in human flesh. He had confidence in all that He represented as the Living Word of God. When preaching in synagogues, Jesus was not surprised when hidden demons screamed out from the lips of their unsuspecting hosts. The Messiah was God's light shining into the dark recesses of secret sins. Just as sudden bright light causes cockroaches to run, so Jesus' words compelled demons to cry out and then flee the scene.

The Lord commissioned His disciples and the seventy, giving them the authority to use His name when ministering to the afflicted. This legacy extends to anyone who confesses Jesus as Lord and Savior.

The following paraphrase is my interpretation of the Lord's commands to us regarding the deliverance ministry. It is composed of excerpts of His words from Matthew 28:18–20 and Mark 16:17–18: "All authority has been given to Me in heaven and on earth. Go therefore and make disciples of all nations, teaching them to observe all things that I have commanded you. And these signs will follow those who believe: In My name they will cast out demons and they will lay hands on the sick, and they will recover."

What About Today?

Although, as we noted earlier, most cultures today maintain some awareness of the presence of evil spirits—creatures with wings and horns, dwarves and goblins and *jinns,* to name just a few—little is generally made of any need for deliverance. Judging from the numbers of people to whom Jesus and His disciples ministered, we might wonder if the need for liberation from demonic powers has shrunk over the past two millennia. Has the number really decreased from "many" in Jesus' day to only a few now?

Clearly, the correct answer is that the number has not diminished. If anything it has increased exponentially, a fact that is apparent with even a casual comparison of the Jewish culture of Jesus' day to modern-day life. In American culture alone the landscape is riddled with satanically inspired, demon-attracting activities that were unimaginable in Israel during the first century—occult movies and TV programs; Internet pornography; anti-biblical philosophies promoted in the educational system.

In contrast to any other nation in the world throughout history, adherence to God-given regulations was central to Jewish culture. Though Israel had a history of rebellion against God, the Torah was the textbook; rabbis ran the schools; fathers taught their sons a trade; wives were stay-at-home moms. People were executed for involvement in occultism, idolatry, premarital sex and similar activities.

In comparison to modern living, their society bore the benchmarks of a godly nation. Yet Jesus and His 41 teams found it necessary to expel demons from normal, productive Jewish people everywhere they went. (Non-Jewish peoples also benefitted from this ministry—such as the Canaanite woman whose daughter was being tortured by a demon. Her story is told in Matthew 15:21–28.)

Ancient Jewish society did not have the high density of God-defying practices that flood most nations of the world today. Even though they were largely protected from demon-attracting societal ills, they were not free from demonic infestations.

This gives us vital insight into the nature of evil spirits. Granted, direct disobedience of godly principles puts out a welcome sign for demonic invasion, but by nature they are ruthless. Wicked spirits do not wait for an obvious invitation; they are spiritual parasites that attack the innocent as well as the wayward.

Types of Demons

The function of all demons is to infiltrate people's lives. The particular drive of a demon is usually revealed in its name. The New Testament mentions a number of evil spirits, and we see that, generally speaking, their names relate to their functions. Most of us have encountered people who might be struggling with these types of manifestations. Note, too, that this list of spirits that are specifically named in the Scriptures is by no means exhaustive. Demons can be the culprits behind any malady of soul or body.

- Jesus dealt with a *spirit of infirmity* that caused a woman to have curvature of the spine (see Luke 13:11–12).
- He expelled a *mute and deaf spirit* from a young boy (see Mark 9:14–27).
- The Lord also rebuked the *fever* that had kept Peter's mother-in-law bedridden (see Luke 4:38–39). The act of rebuking implies the presence of an entity capable of understanding and obeying the dictates of the scolding.
- The apostle Paul cast a *spirit of divination* out of a young woman who earned money for her owners by telling fortunes (see Acts 16:16–19).
- In 1 Timothy 4:1–3, Paul mentioned deceiving spirits that would espouse *false doctrines relating to marriage and diet*. Most of us know men and women who say they want to get

married, but continually break up with hopeful prospects. When asked why, the routine response is, "I just can't commit to a long-term relationship." Some of those people may be influenced by demons that obstruct commitment to marriage. We also likely have friends who are fad-diet buffs. At times their insistence that others adhere to their diets can become uncomfortably intrusive. In such cases, the voice we are hearing might be that of an evil spirit chattering away.

- In 2 Timothy 1:7, Paul spoke of the *spirit of fear*. The word for "fear" can also be translated "timidity." All of us have met unusually shy people who have no obvious reasons to be so. A multitude of phobias—such as claustrophobia, microphobia and obsessive-compulsive disorder—are common manifestations of the spirit of fear.

- In relation to the *spirit of the Antichrist*, the apostle John spoke of the *spirit of error* (see 1 John 4:3–6). The spirit of error causes people to voice acute opposition to any suggestion of the divinity of Jesus of Nazareth. Islam and atheism are two prime examples.

The types and functions of demons also affect how they infiltrate human lives. There are three primary gateways that these demons use: (1) our untempered negative emotions, (2) the aspects of our fallen nature that Paul called "the works of the flesh" and (3) the dangerous path of spiritual adultery. Let's look briefly at each of these.

How Demons Enter Using Our Emotions

Without question, the most common access for evil spirits is through the negative emotions rising from negative dynamics of interpersonal relationships. All human emotions fall roughly within six basic categories. We respond to three positively and three negatively. The positive emotions are love, peace and joy. The negative emotions are anger, fear and pain.

Every emotion evokes corresponding sensations in our souls and bodies. To give an example, think how tension over a domestic situation might cause the muscles in a person's back to stiffen, or it might lead to migraines or depression. For the basis of discussion, let's call this response to our emotions "emotional energy." We welcome the happy emotions of love, peace and joy because they give us pleasurable feelings. We do not welcome anger, fear and pain because they make us feel bad.

Whether positive or negative, our emotions are for our benefit. They help us understand what is going on within us and enable us to respond in some manner to life situations. Our responses to the negative emotions, however, have particular import in the discussion of demons. Dealing in a healthy manner with the energy of negative emotions can help us grow and mature. Suppressing the energy of those negative emotions, however, can wound our souls and bodies (see Proverbs 15:13; 17:22) and open the door to demons.

This is why it is necessary to deal with our negative emotions in a biblical manner, or else we will begin to act in ways that are detrimental to us and displeasing to God—and evil spirits will take advantage of the situation. Anger that is not dealt with welcomes demons of hostility, bickering, violence, retaliation and rebellion. Fear invites demons of anxiety, various phobias, lying, rejection, sexual hang-ups and the like. Emotional pain can attract spirits of depression, defeat, despair, self-pity, escapism and suicide.

Surges of emotion from anger, fear and pain that might cause us to want to strike out are striking inwardly with equal force. These surges can literally be felt throughout our psyches and our bodies. Though we are unaware of what is happening, the sensations of anger, fear and pain are actually pounding our souls. If left unattended day after day, incident after incident, these sensations can give the devil a foothold within us (see Ephesians 4:26–27). Satan does not take up personal residence. He sends one of his demons to nest in the festering wound that the energy of our repeated negative emotions has created within our souls.

How This Process Starts

The process by which demons gain a foothold through our emotions is given in the book of James. We should note that the people to whom James is addressing his letter are Christians.

> But if you have bitter envy and self-seeking in your hearts, do not boast and lie against the truth. This wisdom does not descend from above, but is earthly, sensual, demonic. For where envy and self-seeking exist, confusion and every evil thing are there.
>
> JAMES 3:14–16

These verses speak of the emotions of bitter envy and selfishness. Both can be manifestations of the emotion of anger. An embittered, self-seeking person is angry because he or she perceives others as possessing something he or she does not. The anger begins as an earthly, natural reaction. If allowed to heighten, it will become a preoccupation of the soul and mind.

The word used for such preoccupations is *sensual*. A more accurate translation is *soulish*, pertaining to the soul. Incessant rehearsal of bitter, selfish feelings can wound the soul. If the person does not repent, demons will enter our lives and intensify the anger inherent in those soulish, embittered, self-seeking preoccupations.

Here is an example of how the process works. Say a friend comments with a laugh that it looks as though I have "put on a few extra pounds." My earthly, natural reaction is to shrug it off as inconsequential. Throughout the coming days, however, it returns to my mind, and I begin to think through scenarios about how I will respond the next time he makes weight comments.

At that juncture my natural reaction has spiraled down into a soulish preoccupation. My soul is now being wounded by the sensations of anger that strike it every time I think of him. This is an open invitation for a demon of anger to pounce upon me.

If I do not repent and forgive my friend for his jovial remark, my end condition is to allow that demon of anger to have residence within me. At the mention of my friend's name, my soul and lips go into attack mode. Though I still love my brother in Christ, I shun opportunities to fellowship with him. Unbeknownst to him, I have allowed his lighthearted comment to stir my emotions and to propel me into a state of demonically inspired offense.

Facing the Truth about Ourselves

The verses cited from James speak of a form of misdirected wisdom that can lead to conditions in which demons can torment us. James's words warn us against suppressing how we really feel. Denial is one and the same as lying against the truth. In that regard, believers tend to be the kings and queens of denial. Far too often, we refuse to acknowledge the negative emotions of anger, fear and pain that we feel in our daily lives.

Most Christians are conditioned to be performance-centered. The performance-centered tend to interpret the expression of legitimate emotion as carnality, lack of self-control and the like. Negative emotions can be expressed appropriately by those who are willing to speak the truth in love to those who have brought offense. Not disciplining ourselves to do so opens the gateway for demons to enter our lives.

With this truth in mind, it would behoove us as believers to ask ourselves some hard questions. How many church splits have been spawned by demon-induced squabbles over nonessential doctrines? How many dear Christian friends have been lost due to minor offenses? From a personal perspective, do I express my negative emotions of anger, fear and pain appropriately to those who purposely or unwittingly stir up my emotions? Or do I seethe inside, allowing my emotions to batter my soul day after day?

The way we answer those questions will very likely indicate whether we or other Christians we know are candidates for deliverance related to our emotions.

If you are a candidate, you have nothing to fear or to be ashamed about. It is not a crime to have issues related to demons. It is, however, self-inflicted abuse to suspect demonic activity and not do something about it.

How Demons Infiltrate through the Flesh

The works of the flesh that Paul lists in Galatians 5:18–21 are: adultery, fornication, uncleanness, lewdness, idolatry, sorcery, hatred, contentions, jealousies, outbursts of wrath, selfish ambitions, dissensions, heresies, envy, murders, drunkenness and revelries. Evil spirits can attach to any of these offenses and exacerbate them. There are, for instance, demons of jealousy and selfish ambitions.

In addition, each one of the works of the flesh has correlating sins that spin off from it, and demons can attach to those as well. I refer to such spirits as "spin-off demons." Fornication, for instance, includes spin-off demons of every aberrant sexual practice, including homosexuality.

Lewdness includes spin-off demons such as overt sensuality. A young lady came to me complaining about workplace sexual harassment. As she spoke, I had a vision of several male dogs trailing a female dog that was in heat. Because I did not want to insult the woman, I did not tell her what I saw. I simply asked her if she would be willing to repent of dressing in a sensual manner. She repented tearfully. I commanded the demon of sensuality to leave her. She had no more office difficulties.

Drunkenness includes spin-off demons attached to any addictive substance, such as tobacco. On numerous occasions smokers who could not quit have come to me seeking deliverance. Many have reported complete freedom after I cast the spirit of addiction to nicotine from them.

I am not suggesting, of course, that everyone who exhibits the symptoms of one of these demons is being influenced by that particular entity. Nonetheless, there are millions who do not discern that they have given themselves to works of the flesh, and that they are now being manipulated by more than the routine weakness of being human.

How Demons Enter through Spiritual Adultery

Along with the gateways of our negative emotions and our fallen human nature, we allow invisible enemies to infiltrate our lives through specific choices we make that are in direct conflict with God's laws. Here, we address practices the Bible labels as spiritual harlotry or spiritual adultery. These include idolatry, superstition, the occult, as well as seeking psychic and paranormal experiences. (Uninvited psychic and paranormal experiences are commonplace; seeking them is problematic.) You may experience the conviction of the Holy Spirit as you read. Specific steps to freedom begin in the next chapter.

Occult Practices and Resultant Curses

Involvement with the occult and idolatry brings with it self-inflicted curses and penalties. The curses are often set in motion by demonic entities. A study of the Old Testament reveals two lists pertinent to this topic of spiritual adultery. The first list gives types of occult practices. The second list describes the curses attached to idolatry and occultism. The curses are too numerous to cite. Here we note the most common ones that batter the lives of their victims, describing their effects in contemporary terms.

Keep in mind that evil spirits actually empower the occult practitioners and activate curses in their lives. That is why it is common for those consulting them to become likewise infested by spirits.

To introduce the first list, occult practices, let's look at a helpful passage in Deuteronomy 18:

> "When you come into the land which the LORD your God is giving you, you shall not learn to follow the abominations

of those nations. There shall not be found among you anyone who makes his son or his daughter pass through the fire, or one who practices witchcraft, or a soothsayer, or one who interprets omens, or a sorcerer, or one who conjures spells, or a medium, or a spiritist, or one who calls up the dead. For all who do these things are an abomination to the LORD, and because of these abominations the LORD your God drives them out from before you. You shall be blameless before the LORD your God. For these nations which you will dispossess listened to soothsayers and diviners; but as for you, the LORD your God has not appointed such for you."

DEUTERONOMY 18:9–14

1. *Witchcraft.* This is the attempt to manipulate people and situations through the exertion of the human spirit or demonic spirits. Witchcraft also employs curses, spells, charms and potions. Practitioners sell amulet jewelry charms, spoken charmed incantations and concocted drink potions to customers.

2. *Soothsayer.* Soothsayers claim psychic empowerment. Their abilities are used to gain prophetic insight into hidden matters of the past, present and future.

3. *Sorcerer.* This is a wizard who is consulted to put positive or negative magical spells on unwitting victims. It includes the offering of "blessed" amulets and potions to ward off evil and to ensure health and success.

4. A *medium, spiritist or one who calls up the dead.* This category covers a variety of practices. The first is that of mediums and spiritists. The modern idiom for the way they function is called *channeling.* This is old-fashioned spiritism wherein the information and voices coming through spiritists are alleged to be from the dead. Mediums cannot actually contact the dead. Most of them have one or more evil spirits within them that make contact with the demonic powers that either inhabited or were familiar with the departed (thus their designation as "familiar spirits.")

At times, mediums conduct séances asking for the inquirers to participate. Most often, however, psychic spiritists prefer to put on one-man shows. The most common form of medium activity is through Ouija boards. A participant asks the operative spiritual power in the board (a demon) a question. The planchett pointer under the inquirer's fingers points to letters and numbers spelling out information, or goes to yes and no to answer specific questions.

5. *One who interprets omens.* Those who interpret omens use natural events to predict future events. Divination through tea leaves, palm and Tarot card readings are variations of omen prognostications. Astrologers who chart movements in the heavens to forecast the future are interpreting omens.

We see modern counterparts of these in practitioners of Cuban Santeria, African orisha, Brazilian macumba, Haitian voodoo, aboriginal shamanism and Hispanic curanderoism. Each of these employs mixtures of the practices listed in Scripture.

We draw the second list, the list of curses, from the verses following this warning in Deuteronomy 28:15:

"But it shall come to pass, if you do not obey the voice of the LORD your God, to observe carefully all His commandments and His statutes which I command you today, that all these curses will come upon you and overtake you."

- *Confusion and frustration* in all you attempt to accomplish (see verse 20)
- *Defeat by one's enemies*, humiliation at the hand of competitors (see verse 25)
- *Groping for reasonable prosperity* only to receive significant losses (see verse 29)
- *Children ensnared* by peer pressure contrary to parental values (see verse 32)

- *Chronic sicknesses* for which no remedies are found (see verses 35, 59)

- *Embarrassment about not achieving success levels* common with others who are afforded similar opportunities (see verse 37)

- *Out-of-control indebtedness* when income is sufficient to meet all needs (see verse 44)

- *Hostility from spouses* toward their mates and children (see verses 54–56)

- *Homes, businesses and vehicles repossessed* (see verse 63)

- *Panic attacks, restlessness and insomnia* (see verses 65–66)

- *Dread of day* at night, *dread of night* during the day (see verse 67)

We have all observed good people struggling with one or more of the symptoms of the curses listed. It is not uncommon for those experiencing the symptoms of curses to battle suicidal thoughts. For many, the oppressive circumstances driving them to thoughts of ending their lives are spawned by demons within and without.

As an example, we see a connection of the curse "defeat by one's enemies" (see verse 25) to the life of King Saul, who was wounded in battle and subsequently committed suicide. This is tied specifically to his consultation of a medium (see 1 Samuel 28:7–24; 1 Chronicles 10:4, 13).

A number of other practices fall into the category of spiritual adultery. Here are three.

Astrology

Notable theologian Joseph A. Seiss wrote an inspiring book titled *The Gospel in the Stars*. First published in 1882, his book made the case that constellations and signs of the Zodiac actually support Redemption's story. Seiss's suppositions include historical insights and are well-supported by Bible references. Job, for instance, verified the names and locations of three constellations, the Bear, Orion and

Pleiades (see Job 9:9). The starry hosts symbolically depict the glory and power of the Godhead to all who might look toward the heavens (see Psalm 19:1–6; Romans 1:18–20).

The divine intention for the significance of stars has been polluted by the false assertions of horoscopes and astrology. Probably the greatest lie is that the alignment of the stars identifies character traits and the futures of individuals. Horoscopes are a satanic deception.

The prophet Jeremiah recorded what our attitude should be toward astrological charts: "Thus says the LORD: 'Do not learn the way of the Gentiles; do not be dismayed at the signs of heaven, for the Gentiles are dismayed at them'" (Jeremiah 10:2).

Interest in the Paranormal

All media sources are exploding with occult-related themes. The number of television programs about paranormal activities, such as "investigators" who track sightings, for instance, reveals the unhealthy interest.

A good percentage of the storylines are so much rubbish, by the way. Supposedly, the "things that go bump in the night," the eerie voices and the moving objects are the haunting ghosts of a house's previous occupants. I am convinced that for the most part the paranormal events being filmed are staged. The programming is entertainment for the gullible. It is designed to sell the sponsor's products.

There are, of course, credible reports and sightings. In such instances, it is not ghosts that are present, but rather demons mimicking the dead. The evil spirit(s) causing the disturbances once inhabited a person who lived and died while a resident in whatever building is being affected. Believers have full authority to stop all paranormal activity in their homes.

It is possible for any home to attract paranormal events. That seemed to be the case with a situation I call "A Tale of Two Sisters."

While I was writing this book, I received a call from a woman whom I will call "Sister 1." She was alarmed about supernatural happenings in her home. Her no-nonsense husband had seen an apparition mimicking a relative who had died. The relative had never lived with them. Then, days later, Sister 1 told me that she had seen her cell phone floating in midair in the kitchen between the breakfast counter and the refrigerator. It fell to the floor when she gasped at the sight.

Across town about a month later, the caller's sister, "Sister 2," began to have worse hassles from the same relative's mimicking demon. One day her eleven-year-old and thirteen-year-old sons reported seeing the deceased relative. Earlier the same day, Sister 2 had had several disconcerting experiences. She had painfully struck her head on three different doors in her home, even though she has 20/20 vision. Then when she went to pick up her kids at baseball practice, she was hit in the back of the head by a baseball. The following day, a front wheel of her SUV fell off when she turned into a parking place. All four of the wheel's bolts had broken off as though sawed through with a hacksaw. Evidence was mounting that the demon's intentions at Sister 2's home were less than friendly.

In dealing with this situation, in which a demon was mimicking their dead grandmother, I led both families in appropriate repentance and renunciation. They knew about demons and needed to repent of treating the affair in a light manner. To my knowledge they have not had any further trouble.

Yoga and Martial Arts

Hinduism's yoga and Taoism's and Buddhism's martial arts are in the mix of questionable practices. In some cases, the physical benefits of the exercises associated with these Eastern disciplines can be achieved without participating in any of their religious or mystical applications. In my estimation the risks are too high.

Yoga is said to relax practitioners and to heighten capabilities for greater creativity. It did not do so in India. Prior to the economic boosts from U.S. job outsourcing and piggybacked research on the scientific advancements of Western nations, the yogis got messages leading to worshiping cows, monkeys and rats and to kissing cobras.

Concerning the martial arts, some karate masters teach their students to embrace the powers of animal spirits and magic. To be sure, students who are eager for approval naïvely open themselves to become inhabited by evil spirits and the curses of life they bring.

Just as Jesus ministered to the "many" of His day, so He wants you liberated for His eternal purposes. With these gateways securely closed, you can truly manifest the love, peace and joy of Kingdom living, freed from demonic hindrances that have bogged you down. Such freedom equates to an ever-increasing capacity for you to enjoy being you, and for those around you to enjoy the true you as well.

In the next chapter, we begin the process toward that freedom.

8

Initial Steps to Freedom

Our negative emotions. Sins of the flesh. Spiritual adultery. Any amount of participation, however small, in any gateway activity puts you at risk for demonic opposition and needs to be addressed. If you recognize any attitude or behavior in yourself that you suspect is strongly influenced by a demon, whether it is through a gateway or some other influence, here are initial steps you may want to take before we delve into specific deliverance techniques.

Step One: Discipline

Our first action is discipline. Through the power of Christ, a redeemed person when tempted to sin has the ability to say no. In most instances, believers who choose to be self-disciplined will experience instant dissipation of the temptation.

Unwillingness to enact such discipline, however, can eventually open the door to evil spirits. When that happens, whichever action it was that gave the demons a foothold will usually become exaggerated and difficult to control. We may still have the ability to suppress the compulsion, but pressures from the demonic presence can wear down our resistance.

In such cases, we soon find ourselves mired in a habitual, demon-driven behavior that plagues us with guilt over our failure. When we realize we are fighting a losing battle with discipline, there are only two steps to follow: repentance and deliverance.

Step Two: Repentance

Scripture shows us that repentance is the necessary precursor to deliverance. Without repentance we will not be in the proper place to be set free from any holds that evil spirits have gained.

Look at the strategic role John the Baptist played in relation to the ministry of Jesus. John the Baptist drew huge crowds from Jerusalem, Judea and all of the surrounding regions. He was speaking of Jesus when he admonished the multitudes to "Repent, for the Kingdom of heaven is at hand!" Thousands were baptized, signaling they had indeed repented of their sins (see Matthew 3:1–6).

Repentance loosened the grip of the demons. When those individuals were then exposed to the ministry of Jesus, the power of repentance was already working within them. Any indwelling evil spirits readily came out as Jesus and His disciples told them to leave.

Repentance shows that we are taking responsibility for our transgressions—even those actions that are promoted by evil spirits. That is to say, God is not impressed with the whimper, "The devil made me do it." The human spirit has the power to resist. Demons are strong, but their compulsions can be quenched by the determined choice of one's personal spirit.

Is it hard? Yes! Is it life-threatening? No! It is an absolute necessity, therefore, for anyone seeking deliverance to take responsibility and repent for giving in to satanically inspired behavior. Suppose we offer Jesus our heartfelt repentance, but fall into the sin again? Suppose that happens over and over? Do we continue to repent? Yes.

God always forgives. When our hearts condemn us, He is greater and more forgiving than our hearts (see 1 John 3:20–21).

When deliverance follows repentance, the repentance will have performed another marvelous function. When a demon exits a person whom he considers his "house," the vacated "house" becomes clean and orderly. If the person who was delivered has truly exercised godly repentance, the spiritual realm within is kept in impeccable condition by the presence of Christ within. Even though an evil spirit craves to reenter his former house with a gang of more wicked spirits, it cannot do so.

Step Three: Deliverance

If we are dealing with a demon, then true repentance for our sin is just the first installment of what we need. In order to get a demonically energized problem to come under control, the demon that intensifies the sin must be expelled.

Specifics for this expelling begin in chapter 9, "Self-Deliverance," and continue throughout the book.

Step Four: Cleaning Your House of Occult Items

The New Covenant releases believers from the obligation to comply with most of the laws of the Old Covenant. Nevertheless, there are some Old Testament laws that carry over into the New Covenant. God is jealous for our affection and our loyalty. The following verse emphasizes that in God's sight, past and present engagement in pagan practices is idolatry: "My people consult their wooden idol, and their diviner's wand informs them; for a spirit of harlotry has led them astray, and they have played the harlot, departing from their God" (Hosea 4:12, NASB).

Christians are told in 1 Corinthians 10:14 to flee from idolatry. The believers at Ephesus exemplified what "fleeing idolatry" entails. It is apparent many of the new Ephesian converts had continued to dabble with the mystical aspects of their culture after coming to Christ. When they discovered the danger of doing so, they confessed the practice as sin and demonstrated their repentance by bringing their books on the magical arts to be burned in the presence of the apostles. Others possessing household images of the goddess Diana destroyed those statues. The craftsmen who sculpted the shrines became highly agitated, fearing their livelihoods would be threatened by the masses coming to faith in Jesus Christ.

The incident that precipitated this burning of occult materials and the destruction of idols was the failure of Jewish exorcists to deliver a demonized man. Sceva, a chief priest of Judaism, had seven sons who were exorcists. They attempted to incorporate the name of Jesus into their exorcism incantations. The demon recognized that the men did not have a relationship with Christ. Not only did it refuse their commands to depart from its host, it empowered the afflicted man with superhuman strength so that he physically assaulted all seven of the exorcists and put them to flight (see Acts 19:11–20, 23–28).

The failure of the exorcists to liberate the man (along with the physical beating the demon prompted) frightened the superstitious Christians of Ephesus. It demonstrated how powerless the traditional magical arts were against forces of evil. In fact, it showed that the use of magical incantations to repulse evil spirits actually gave the entities stronger footholds! As a result, believers at Ephesus repented and destroyed their occult materials.

These verses in Deuteronomy further state the case for getting rid of occult items:

> "You shall burn the carved images of their gods with fire; you shall not covet the silver or gold that is on them, nor take it for yourselves, lest you be snared by it; for it is an abomination to the LORD your God. Nor shall you bring an abomination into your house, lest you be doomed to destruction like it. You shall utterly detest it and utterly abhor it, for it is an accursed thing."

DEUTERONOMY 7:25–26

The works of darkness have not ceased over the millennia: Evil practices and curses are rampant today, though not all are as blatant as sorcery and witchcraft. Often works of evil make their way into people's lives in the guise of accepted behavior, even among Christians. Take an inventory of your home. Is it adorned with pagan idols like Buddhas, art pieces like fertility gods and occult knickknacks like good-luck charms? If so, this indicates strong attachments to idolatrous art and to the occult.

The following testimony from a close friend confirms the importance of destroying occult items.

One night some years ago, a brother in the Lord phoned from Atlanta, Georgia, at around two A.M. Let me begin by saying that all in his family were well-educated, dignified Christians with no tolerance for superstition.

This night he was alarmed by something bizarre that was taking place right at that moment in his home. He had just been awakened by strange, guttural sounds coming from the bedroom formerly occupied by his daughter, who was now married and living elsewhere.

He went in to find his wife lying on the floor of that room in what appeared to be a catatonic state, her mouth opened wide and issuing these sounds. Suddenly, the growls from his wife's throat changed into hateful statements about their son-in-law. My friend told me that he could not figure out how she could articulate intelligible words without moving her lips, but that was what was taking place.

At my instruction, he bound the evil spirit of hatred speaking through his wife. The speech stopped, but intermittent growls continued to resound in her abdominal area and out through her throat.

All attempts to awaken her from her stupor failed. Even stranger, while this man was on the phone with me, he said he was hearing strange fluttering noises and owl hoots coming from his front and back lawns. He left the phone to investigate. He was astonished to discover that dozens of owls had descended on their property. They were dolefully "who-whoing" as they fluttered from tree to tree. (Owls are an ancient symbol of hidden wisdom.)

As we talked further he told me that their daughter, while in college, had pledged to a sorority whose mascot and symbol was an owl. The pledge invoked the wisdom of owls for success in life. This young lady had been married for years to her college sweetheart and co-worker with Campus Crusade for Christ. After marriage, she had left her collection of owls to decorate nearly every nook and cranny of her parents' home.

I led my friend in a renunciation of any curses instigated by his financing of his daughter's ill-advised pledge and her fetish with owl collecting. He did so and began to destroy the figurines. During the process, his wife slipped into peaceful slumber.

The next sign of progress was that the owls flew off during our conversation, and he has not seen any owls in the vicinity of his property since that night. Later, his wife received full deliverance from her animosities toward her son-in-law.

Months later, my friend told me that his daughter began to instigate uncharacteristic arguments with her husband. During that time, she attended a deliverance conference and went forward for ministry. The meetings took place while Derek Prince's first wife, Lydia, was still alive, and Lydia ministered to her.

When the daughter opened up to Lydia about her marital problems, Lydia asked if the young woman had ever had any contact with the occult. She told Lydia of the owl incident with her mother and her own pledge to a sorority honoring the owl as its symbol.

Lydia led her through a renunciation of the sorority oath and encouraged her to get rid of any affiliated items. The young woman was wearing her sorority ring, an owl-shaped diamond cluster. She took it off and threw it into the trash. The affiliated demon was commanded to come out of her, and it did. Subsequently, her relational troubles subsided.

How to Clean House

In general, cleansing a home of anything related to idolatry and the corresponding evil spirits is a simple procedure. If children are present, the parents should gather the family to explain what has been happening and what is to be done about it. The process should be relaxed without any sense of fear or alarm.

First, all the family should join in a prayer of repentance from and renunciation of any preoccupation with any form of idolatry. This might include interest in paranormal literature, movies, TV programs, websites or computer games. The family head leads the family in repentance, the family reciting the words during the leader's pauses.

They should then renounce curses. The family head again leads the family in prayer. The prayer might be something like this: "Father, we renounce any type of physical, emotional or financial curse penalty that came upon any member of our household for dabbling in forbidden areas." (Describe any known specific consequences: financial problems, unending medical issues, incessant child-parent squabbles, etc.)

Next, all should go room by room commanding any demons to leave the family's bodies and lives in Jesus' name.

Finally, if there are any articles in the home that represent idolatry, they should be destroyed.

Most of the time one cleansing session is effective. At times a repeat cleansing may be necessary, and the process should be repeated as before.

If you are the one who has allowed demonic entry into your home by your personal practices, you can follow the steps for cleaning house privately. If you have been reciting mantras while doing yoga, for instance, quit both. If you are into karate, aikido or jujitsu and practice any of the spiritual applications, repent, renounce and quit.

Helping Others

If you know people who have occult items in their homes, you might wonder whether or not to broach the subject. My personal policy is to remain quiet about this, unless they want to talk about problematic situations they are facing. In that case, I share the concepts of these chapters. My objective is to persuade them to repent and to banish the defiling items from their homes.

If you find that you are in regular contact with someone who has opened the gateways to invisible enemies, and you feel that you should address the situation, remember that the conversation of Christians is to be seasoned with the salt of grace. We must approach both the unconverted and the believers we consider to be in error in a gracious and redemptive manner. Rather than make hurtful and inflammatory comments, we need to recognize that their interest in idolatrous items and occult material may actually be a cloaked, albeit misdirected, longing to experience the Kingdom of God. Believers should respond with grace and understanding when listening to others as they speak of their spiritual journeys. Only after listening politely will we be in a position to offer biblical options that can better satisfy their thirst for supernatural experiences.

Here is the main point, whether the need is for you or for someone who has come to you for help: After acknowledging the particular sinful involvement, repentance and renunciation are necessary for any needed deliverance to take place.

A Word about Children

Special cautions need to be exercised when dealing with children and teens. Most of us do not live in closed religious communities like the Amish or Hassidic Jewish families. Inevitably, our children will have interaction with children whose parents do not share our values. The peer pressure on them can be formidable, since our children may not be permitted to read popular books, listen to the latest musical groups or play questionable computer games.

For the parent, harping is counterproductive. As parents, we need to evaluate when to yield and when to stand our ground. Our God is gracious. The passing fads of Harry Potter books and rock music do not represent the same level of danger as séances, Ouija boards and demonic role-playing games. Parents ought to explain any necessary prohibitions without any sense of alarm, and in a manner appropriate to a particular child's age and temperament. With teens, it is prudent to lay out the case for nonparticipation and then let them make their own decisions.

I know of many Christian parents who have handled this sensitive area in this way. Their kids made it through the minefields of their teen years without incurring infestations by demons of the occult. I also know of parents who issued prohibitions at fever pitch. Sadly, many of their kids rebelled and opened themselves to the very practices the parents were so strenuously prohibiting.

There is another factor to consider. You can be assured that whatever you say to your kids about demons, curses, Satan and similar subjects will reach the ears of adults who do not understand. That is all the more reason to monitor the intensity of what we say, so they do not encounter unwarranted criticism. I am not suggesting that we should compromise essential tenets of our beliefs. I am suggesting that it is best to pursue peace and not set up our children (and ourselves) for unnecessary controversy.

If Your Family Objects

If you have family members who are less spiritually aware, act judiciously about house cleansings. Never act rashly. You must be careful about destroying family items that are jointly owned. The ideal approach is to wait for a relaxed setting to discuss what you have discovered. When you sense the moment is right, state your desires to discard certain objects and books. If you approach others on the basis that you understand your request sounds strange, but to be patient with you, most will respond reasonably. In other words, the request can be, "Will you let me do it for my sake?"

If the answer is no, it is better not to make an issue of the matter. Let it go. God knows your heart and you have done all that you can do without making Him the family's enemy. Most times, there will be no spiritual repercussions when you are submissive to the sensitivities of a marriage partner.

The prophet Elisha was used of God to heal the heathen officer Naaman of leprosy. Naaman repented of and renounced his former idolatries. There were, however, extenuating circumstances: Naaman was required to accompany the king of Syria as he worshiped the false god Rimmon. It was Naaman's responsibility to steady the king's hand as he bowed to the idol, which necessitated that Naaman also bow before it. Elisha told Naaman not to be concerned about the matter and to go in God's peace (see 2 Kings 5:17–19).

We can believe God for the same latitude. Your private repentance and renunciation will be fruitful. You have done all that you can do to break relations with the world of the occult and false religions. God knows your circumstances and will graciously give you deliverance and peace from all curses and demonic attachments.

Chapter 9 will help you diagnosis whether or not you need deliverance. It will also walk you through the self-deliverance process.

9

Self-Deliverance

There are no sure-fire formulas to identify what gives demons entrance into people's lives. While we usually find dots connecting sin to affliction from evil spirits, it is possible that there can be instances of affliction that have no traceable path to sin. Be that as it may, the failure to confess known sins prior to deliverance can frustrate attempts to expel evil spirits.

In addition, believers are God's representatives. Even as He forgives our sins against Him, we are to forgive the sins of others toward us. Jesus warned that unforgiving people would be turned over to the torturers. It is probable that the tormenters to whom Jesus referred were symbolic of evil spirits (see Matthew 18:34–35). Many who come for deliverance stubbornly holding on to grudges have already experienced demonic torture. Their condition will continue until they make the decision to forgive everyone who has offended them.

As you begin the process of self-deliverance, you can ask yourself some helpful questions to diagnose areas where you might have powers of darkness lurking. The material below will help you consider several categories that are often nesting places for invisible enemies.

It will ask you pertinent questions and suggest the names of related demons. This is based on material you have already studied in this book. This is not an exhaustive list; it is designed to prime the pump of your thinking. Take notes, as you will use them later.

The most reliable Person to help in this endeavor is the Holy Spirit. Ask Him to bring to mind any other areas not listed here where you might need help. Let the Spirit of God within you pose the right questions. If your answers suggest the presence of an evil spirit, ask Him to give you the name or function of the particular demon involved. Identify the evil spirits you suspect by names denoting their functions.

After you have prayerfully considered the categories and their questions, you will be directed to go through the preliminary steps of repentance and renunciation of known sins. Then refer to your list and command the demons to leave you one by one. I have provided three interrelated prayers that affirm your authority over the enemy. Within a few minutes, you can be liberated from your uninvited passengers.

Category Questions

Here, then, are questions in various categories to help you get started, followed by the process of self-deliverance.

Motivation

Why do you want to be set free? While it is legitimate to seek deliverance for your own welfare, there are higher reasons in God's economy. Are you willing to use your new liberty to serve the purposes of God's Kingdom and to bless those whose lives you touch? If not, spirits of pride and self-centeredness might be the problem.

Addiction Issues

Are there particular sins, habits and practices to which you feel enslaved? Do you find yourself repeatedly committing those sins regardless of your efforts to stop? Vulgar and profane language, pornography, compulsive lying and any habits harmful to your body are examples of this problem. Out-of-bounds sexual practices, drugs, alcohol and tobacco can all have attached spirits of addiction. Lying and obscene expletives are often demonic compulsions.

Relationships

Are you plagued with problems in your interpersonal relationships? That is often a common arena for demonic activity. Evil spirits have humanlike psychological characteristics and emotions. They possess intelligence and the ability to communicate. Demons use those capacities to project their perverted emotions of anger, fear and pain into the souls of those whom they inhabit. Their intelligence enables them to pinpoint the weaknesses and emotional wounds of their hosts.

Evil spirits are restless. They cannot endure a host having productive, deep, enduring relationships. Once again, the intelligence of demons and their familiarity with the host equips them to know opportune buttons to push to insert their negative thoughts. Demons do so in every aspect of life including marriage, parent-child relationships, vocational settings and church relationships. Their objective is to influence those they inhabit to wander restlessly from relationship to relationship seeking satisfaction and not finding it.

Do you have a history of broken relationships? Are there people who have wronged you whom you have not forgiven? Is anger, fear or pain nearly always lurking beneath the surface as you interact with certain people? Do you anticipate rejection rather than acceptance when contemplating visits with family and friends of the past? Are you fearful about making new friends? Do you desire to cultivate meaningful relationships, yet find yourself seeking isolation more than fellowship?

In such cases, evil spirits of unforgiveness, rejection, alienation, fear, anger and divorce are common. People who wander from one marriage to the next are frequently inhabited by spirits of adultery, hatred of men or hatred of women. Nomadic demons drive people from one job site to the next.

The Occult

Occult spirits do not normally become embedded in people whose contact with pagan mysticism and cultural idolatry is restricted to academic studies. Problems typically arise from a more deliberate pursuit, such as consulting a psychic for guidance. The potential for demonization is multiplied when a person adopts psychic practices in order to give guidance to others. Operating Ouija boards, role-playing as demons in games and participating in séances are particularly problematic.

Have you ever consulted a spiritist, a medium, a fortune-teller or a Ouija board for personal guidance? Do you follow horoscopes? Have you actively attempted to cultivate psychic abilities? Do you call upon the dead for guidance? Is there a familiar spirit you invite to use you as a channel when others ask for advice? Is there something within you that drives you to want to control those around you to the extent that you have been called a control freak? Is your home decorated with images of idolatrous worship? Do you have a library of occult books?

With all of these questions in mind, consider one more: Are there any previously rare sins, sicknesses, relational difficulties or vocational stresses that have evolved in your life subsequent to your occult interests? If so, the hindrances have little chance of stopping until you repent and renounce the sin of spiritual adultery. If you have answered yes to any of these questions, it is possible you are hosting evil spirits. Demons of divination, manipulation, control and witchcraft are among the usual suspects.

Curses

The three major reasons people are cursed are direct disobedience of God's Word, willful rejection of personal conscience and rebellion against God-ordained authority figures.

Curses are planted by sowing seeds of disobedience. Demons facilitate the way those crops are reaped. I believe God allowed for this negative alternative to the principle of sowing and reaping in the human experience as a deterrent to sin. Once the wise understand the principle of sowing and reaping, they will heed the caution not to sin.

Have you purposely rejected the counsel of your conscience by doing things you know should not be done? Have you defiantly rebelled against God's will and against those with legitimate authority in your life? Did your once-loving spouse suddenly become hostile toward all you represent? Have your hopes of vocational success continually been shattered? Do you continually struggle in your finances, even though your income is sufficient? Do you wrestle with fear at night concerning the day to follow? During the day do you long for the escape of night? Have you helplessly watched your children develop attitudes and friendships that make it almost impossible for you to enjoy them? Do you have physical pain and sickness for which no remedy seems to work?

Some of the evil spirits that energize the curses implied in these questions are rebellious disrespect, verbal abuse, failure, hopelessness, poverty, pain and infirmity.

The Mind

God is not the author of confusion. It is His will for you to be free from anxiety. When conversing with others, do you get confused and have trouble staying on the topic? Does the fear of saying something wrong hinder you from offering your helpful perspectives? Do you have paralyzing fears about routine events of life that others take in stride? Are you hindered from multitasking because you repeatedly redo a single task? Do you have compulsive fixations about cleanliness and the presence of germs? Are you plagued with concerns about people harboring evil intentions against you? Do you take narcotics to numb anxiety? Do you fear losing contact with reality? Is there a history of mental illness in your family?

These questions expose the possible presence of demons of confusion, schizophrenia, paranoia and various compulsive disorders.

Sexuality

After the creation of the first man and woman, God looked upon all He had created and approved all of it as good. The good included the capacity to enjoy sex. The physical union of a husband and wife symbolizes the joy inherent in God's spiritual union with the redeemed. Satan hates God for choosing mankind rather than him for participation in the divine nature; therefore, Satan assigns demons to defile the act of marriage.

Sex is designed to be one of many pleasurable aspects of life. The devil's goal is to pervert that which God designed as good, and drive people to be obsessed with sex as though it were the only important aspect of life.

Are you preoccupied with sex to the extent that other aspects of life lack your attention? Do you have concerns about homosexual, incestuous or pedophilic fixations? Have you ever engaged in any of those activities? Do you fantasize about any of them while masturbating? Are you guilty of multiple premarital and extramarital affairs? Do you frequently visit pornographic websites featuring deviant sex acts? Have you dulled your sensitivities about engaging in certain sex acts that your conscience initially forbade?

The aberrant practices that come to mind with these questions are well-known in many societies. To identify the demons involved, call the acts by their common descriptive names, for example, lust, premarital sex, pornography.

What to Expect

You are on the brink of getting rid of uninvited enemies you have carried for a long while. The manner in which those evil spirits depart may be a jolt to your senses because of the newness of the experience. You have nothing to fear. Any demons that might inhabit you have already done the worst they can do. As you cooperate with the Holy Spirit in expelling them, they have already been weakened by the power of your authority as a child of God.

Please let me emphasize again that authentic deliverance sessions have nothing in common with Hollywood's exorcisms. If, however, you are concerned about what might happen to you on your own, it is fine for you to wait on deliverance until you can make an appointment with someone competent to minister to you. But let me encourage you that you have the ability and authority in Jesus Christ to expel the demons you have identified as troubling you.

While experiencing deliverance, it is important to keep certain factors in mind. The Greek word for *spirit* in the term *evil spirit* is *pneuma*. Its definition means wind, air and breath. Though demons are neither breath nor wind, they often come out through the breath of the mouth in the form of yawns, sighs, huffs, coughs and occasional screams.

Do not be alarmed about hacking coughs or any oral or nasal emissions of mucus. Just think of it in terms of similar reactions you experience with the flu or allergies. The coughs and emissions associated with flu and allergies indicate you are getting rid of something. In deliverance, it is bad stuff out, good stuff in. You will definitely feel and act better within moments of experiencing the manifestations. The evil spirits are being expelled, and you are filling the vacuum within your soul with the presence of the Holy Spirit.

You need to be determined in your efforts, setting your will against the powers of darkness. As a sign of that resolve while expelling them, you can forcefully huff or cough using your lungs, your diaphragm and abdominal area. The action is similar to forceful exhalations of tobacco smoke. One or two determined exhalations are usually sufficient to expel each demon. (Frantic breathing in and out can induce hyperventilation.)

After commanding a particular evil spirit to leave, give it adequate time to exit. Refrain from additional talk between breaths as you expel the spirit. You can pray and give additional commands mentally without actually speaking.

After people have experienced deliverance, some ministers insist upon an intense regimen of Bible reading, prayer and praise—almost in a superstitious manner—to avoid reentry of demons. I do not share their concerns. I prefer that the delivered person assume an assertive posture about the benefits of having the power of Christ and His Holy Spirit abiding within. The person who takes that approach will tend to develop a devotional life that produces intimate fellowship with the Lord through prayer and Bible reading.

My advice to you is to cultivate a devotional life that satisfies the Lord's longing to have fellowship with you. Once you have been delivered, the awareness that your relationship with the Lord is mutually satisfying for you and for Him will keep old passengers at bay.

Now that you understand what to expect as your deliverance takes place, let's begin the process.

The Self-Deliverance Process

1. Take your notes from the diagnostic questions and make a list of the sins you need to repent of and renounce. Also make a list of any demons and curses you suspect.

2. Begin with this prayer of confession of Jesus as Lord in which you will also repent for and renounce all known ties with the occult, and offer prayers of forgiveness.

    "Heavenly Father, I come to You in Jesus' name. I believe Jesus is Your divine Son who died for my sins. I know that You raised Him from the dead. I now call upon the name of Jesus to free me from Satan and sin. I ask You to forgive all of my sins. I declare that because of Your forgiveness, I am a child of God. Satan has no place in me and no unsettled claims against me. All that my life represents now belongs to God and is dedicated to serving His purposes. My spirit, soul and body are the temple of the Holy Spirit, redeemed and cleansed by the blood of

Jesus. I now repent of my sins (name them). I renounce all of the works of darkness associated with the occult. In particular I renounce participation in (name the activities in which you have indulged). I will destroy any literature and images associated with any form of idolatry in which I have participated. From this time forward I am dead to the occult realm and it is dead to me. I will get my guidance from the Word of God, from the Holy Spirit within, from His spiritual revelatory gifts and from godly counsel. Father God, I forgive all who have sinned against me, even as You have forgiven my sins against You. I forgive (name the people) for the way they hurt me. Lord, I bless You and thank You for my salvation and deliverance. In Jesus' name, Amen."

3. Continue by reciting the following prayer for release from curses:

    "At Calvary, Jesus bore all of the curses due me that I might enjoy all of the blessings due Him. I now renounce and separate myself from the curse of (describe whatever the particular curse has done in your life). Those whom the Son has made free are free indeed. I am no longer under any curses. My heritage is the blessing that speaks well of God's loving care and the benefits of being a member of His family. In Jesus' name, Amen."

4. Continue with the following prayer to expel the demon. If you suspect more than one, name and expel them one by one. Do not fret about calling the evil spirit by its exact name. The Holy Spirit knows who and what you are after, and so does the evil spirit. If you do not know its specific name, describe its function and command it to leave you. (For example: "You demon that incites me to use filthy and profane expletives, I command you to leave me now in Jesus' name.") Demons have no choice but to exit as you command them to leave in Jesus' name.

    "Lord Jesus, You said that believers have authority over all of the powers of the enemy and that we are to cast out demons. Your Word says that when we resist

Satan, he will flee from us. On the authority of Your Word, I bind every demonic spirit within me. I command (name or describe the function of one spirit) to come out of me now in Jesus' name."

Keep after each spirit until you have a tangible sense of release. Then go on to the next one on your list.

5. After the session has ended, spend time in thanksgiving to the Lord for the deliverance you have received. You have experienced a miracle. The natural response for such a wonderful gift is to thank the Giver.

Once you have spent ample time thanking the Lord for His deliverance, you will be ready to move on. The deliverance process can be likened to peeling an onion layer by layer. That has certainly been the case with me. But every person is unique and your experience may be totally different from mine or others. Many people go through a single session like that which you have just experienced, are completely freed from demonic trouble and never need another session. Whatever our individual personalities might require, one truth is preeminent: We can give all the glory to God for whatever happens, for He is on our side. He is our Strong Deliverer.

PART TWO

The Next Step
toward Freedom

Now that you understand the process of deliverance, you are ready to take the next step. In the chapters that follow we learn more about the deliverance ministry itself. We look at basic ministries of the Church and see how they partner with deliverance. We uncover various difficulties inherent in deliverance. Plus, we will deal with some subtle devices of the enemy.

Whether you desire to go further in your own self-deliverance or you find yourself in a position to use the techniques in the book to help someone else, let me encourage you that you have the ability and authority in Jesus Christ to expel any invisible enemies you might encounter in your Christian walk. Understanding these basics of deliverance ministry will help you grow in confidence. In Part 3 we go deeper into specific deliverance techniques.

10

Biblical Truth and Human Understanding

The Holy Spirit has inserted an ebb-and-flow dynamic into periods of refreshing the Church. It seems that widespread interest in any rediscovered biblical truth ebbs after a sufficient number of people have grasped it and benefited from it.

Spiritual warfare and demonology as popular conference themes have been at an ebb for a number of years. During this low-tide season, the Lord has been helping us refine doctrines and methodologies pertaining to the deliverance ministry. It has undergone examination in retrospect to discern what is biblical and what is not, what works and what does not, and which practices should be retained and which should be cast aside as excessive. Along the way the Holy Spirit has been giving ongoing revelation to help produce optimal results.

God's desire, I believe, is for deliverance to be fully restored to the Church's weaponry and activated in the purest possible form. A "tsunami" of revival is about to take place, and the Lord is preparing His Body to minister to those who will be ushered into the Kingdom as a result.

Though this process of refining carries with it some high rewards, it is quite challenging. Why? Because Christians tend to be unrealistic about the potential to be deceived themselves. Many assume that errors in doctrine and ministry applications are easy to recognize. They are not.

Deception usually takes a subtle route into general practice. Faithful servants of God, for instance, can dispense deception. They have no idea that what they are saying contains elements of error. Audiences who embrace those errors do so without much question because the teachers have well-earned reputations for advocating biblical truth.

To understand and guard against error, it is essential to know the differences between absolutes and variables in ministry.

Absolutes and Variables

Regarding the ministry of deliverance, there are few biblical absolutes and many experiential variables. Absolutes are the cumulative principles that the Bible teaches us about Satan, demons, incidents of deliverance and related topics. An example of absolutes would be the fact that Jesus cast out demons, or that He defeated Satan at the cross.

Variables, on the other hand, rely on discernment and interpretation. These could be, for instance, any specific occurrences during deliverance or what those in ministry observe while setting the captives free. Doctrinal interpretation, which carries potential for error, is another variable. An example of this would be Jesus' ministry to the demoniac who lived in tombs. That is the only incident in Scripture in which Jesus asked a demon to name itself. Thus, on occasion it is appropriate for those ministering to do so. An error would be insistence that deliverance protocol demands conversing with demons to get their identities. We will discuss variables further in the next chapter.

One classic mistake that Christians in ministry make is to interpret variables as absolutes and absolutes as variables. A particular experience while ministering to one person should not be set in stone as an absolute when ministering to another person.

Satan and his demons are clever. Unquestionably, the devil loses ground whenever evil spirits are expelled. Satan's countering scheme to regain lost ground is to introduce error. It succeeds when protocols of ministry are established on variable ministry experiences rather than the absolutes of sound biblical principles—and even common sense.

Let me give you an example from my own ministry. It has to do with the error of obtaining information in the process of deliverance from the demons that are being expelled. As a preface to what I am about to share, let me state unequivocally that demons cannot be trusted as they are under the command of the father of lies, the devil. Even though I knew this biblical truth, I let error slip in the door.

During the Jesus Movement I often ministered deliverance to the hippies who were coming to Christ in our city. On one occasion, a young woman was having an unusually difficult struggle to find relief. Suddenly, a demonic spirit spoke repeatedly through her lips: "It's the crucifix that keeps me in. I will not go. Her necklace gives me a right to stay."

My reaction was instantaneous and strong: "Get that thing off of your neck now!"

The young lady pulled off the necklace, gasped violently and then breathed a sigh. "It's gone. I'm free. Thank You, Jesus. Thank You, Jesus," she cried.

With a bolstered sense of authority, I instructed her: "From this day forward, don't ever wear a crucifix again. The Lord is no longer hanging on a cross. He has triumphed over the devil and has paid the price for you to enjoy freedom from hassles with evil spirits. You don't need a religious relic to ward off evil."

Ironically, although the young woman was gloriously liberated, I slipped into a form of religious bondage that took months to discern. My success with her led me to believe that religious jewelry gave evil spirits a right to remain in their hosts. I ritualized its removal and destruction whenever I ministered deliverance. The second of the Ten Commandments was my proof text: "You shall not make for yourself a carved image—any likeness of anything that is in heaven above, or that is in the earth beneath, or that is in the water under the earth" (Exodus 20:4).

A Welcome Correction

God was merciful to me and those to whom I ministered. People continued to receive liberation through my prayers, even though a portion of my methodology was off base. After a while, some persons receiving ministry wisely began to resist my assertions that all religious articles must be destroyed. They understood that fetish attachment to just about any object has the potential to strengthen demons, but they also knew they were not guilty of fetishism. I was rescued by several respected leaders who voiced concerns that my position on the wearing of religious objects was excessive.

When I took the time to do some research in the Scriptures on the subject of images, to my chagrin, I found that gifted artisans had been filled with the Spirit to mold images of living things. The decorations of the Tabernacle of Moses and Solomon's Temple consisted of figures of flowers, lions, oxen and cherubim (see Exodus 25:33; 35:30–35; 1 Kings 7:28–29).

I repented of my naïve excessiveness. Through the words of a demon I had heard during deliverance, I had allowed Satan to hoodwink me into making a variable an absolute. Undoubtedly, the hippie girl to whom I was ministering had an inordinate attachment to her crucifix. In her specific, isolated case, it was necessary for her to remove the item in order to be set free. But the truth is, most people can be set free regardless of what Christian symbols they might be wearing.

Ironically, I came into contact with some fellow ministers who refused to lay aside that particular position that I had previously and erroneously held. I attempted to reason with them, but to no avail. For them, their success in ministry equaled God's approval. Their determined stand played right into Satan's strategy to regain ground by diminishing the credibility of their ministries.

I later learned that those brothers had gone into even further excesses about the matter of idolatrous images. Family photographs, for instance, were added to their lists of forbidden paraphernalia. Those dear men ministered publicly for a few years and then were sidelined. In essence, it was deception about the nature of idolatry that shut down their effectiveness in ministry.

The devil has a knack for accentuating the overstatements of preachers in the minds of listeners. Eventually errors of overemphasis can become empowered with lives of their own. The enthusiastic followers of a given preacher can begin to promote his unintentional overstatements as though they were absolutes. In most instances, when reputable teachers learn of such happenings, they instantly make corrective adjustments. At times, however, this can happen after their lives have ended. In that event, the Lord raises up other ministers to make the necessary adjustments. The pull between established partial truths and the effort needed to correct them are a kind of necessary tension keeping the Body of Christ both functional and mobile.

Misapplications and misinterpretations can divert any ministry from its God-ordained focus. In the chapter to come, we will uncover a number of spin-off misconceptions that have evolved from overstated truths about deliverance from evil spirits.

Separating Ministry Chaff
from Wheat

Jesus spoke spiritual truths with undiluted purity. After His ascension into heaven, the truths that the Holy Spirit has revealed to His Church have passed repeatedly through the sieve of human personality. This means that any one of the truths the Lord has intended to instill within His people has the potential to be blurred or altered by doctrinal interpretations and personal experiences. Recognizing this reality, we also recognize that truth is progressive, requiring that we "rediscover" it on a regular basis.

Five Areas of Chaff

Wisdom dictates that those who want to understand—particularly those who practice—any ministry should periodically separate human-generated chaff from the Holy Spirit's genuine wheat. Here are five prevalent chaff-ridden concepts that we need to winnow from our experience and practice of deliverance.

The Concern about Manifestations

Critics have a common complaint about deliverance. They object on the grounds that the Holy Spirit would not make a Christian display undignified manifestations. I agree. I do not believe the Holy Spirit makes people react in peculiar ways. I have come to understand that manifestations during deliverance are combinations of natural physiological responses and the antics of departing demons.

Evil spirits consider their human hosts their personal homes. The resistance of some demons to eviction has similarities to people who feel their landlords are evicting them unjustly. Hardly anyone would fail to express consternation if a landlord came suddenly to throw them out. Many would cry out and make threatening physical gestures. That is precisely what is happening when some demons are confronted with the authority of God's Word during deliverance.

The bodies of believers belong to Jesus, the most powerful of all landlords. Evil spirits are illegal squatters. Demonic entities with strong roots in a person do not leave without a fight. They are apt to express some type of agitated actions as they unwillingly vacate their hosts. On the other hand, many demons have weak personalities. They are not predisposed to make a big fuss, and they simply vacate the premises when commanded to do so.

Not every response is from a demon, of course. Still, the natural physiological responses that some people exhibit during deliverance are often mistakenly attributed to demons. The Lord has designed the human body to have physiological responses to the pleasures and pressures of life. It is not unusual for the stout of heart to get choked up by a "tearjerker" movie. Some people swoon and collapse at the sight of blood. Those who are stressed-out often grind their teeth at night. When long-term emotional issues are relieved, it is not just the sentimental at heart who need tissues to wipe tear-filled eyes and runny noses.

People who have been subjected to long-standing demonic affliction are under incredible emotional pressure. Those with heinous compulsions have constant worries of discovery. People with spirits of rejection are haunted by fears of saying or doing something objection-able. Those who have demonically induced habits such as nail biting are embarrassed when they are detected in the behavior by onlook-ers. Christians of sensitive conscience continually battle to suppress demonic thoughts and inclinations. We have all heard expressions like this: "I'm so frustrated I could scream." Those pent-up screams are resident in the bodies and minds of many people.

When demons are expelled, emotional steam is released from pressure-cooked lives. The lid is lifted from suppressed emotions, and sensations of relief flood through bodies. The natural physiological responses are diverse. The held-back screams escape. Inhibitions are set aside, sometimes involuntarily, as people shake, swoon, moan and weep openly. Uncontrollable laughter is a common physiological response to the release of tension that is far from humorous. I once saw an eight-year-old girl laugh and shake for over an hour. She was being liberated from the terrors that had accumulated within her during the years that she had watched her father dying of cancer.

Is not the Body of Christ an appropriate setting for people to find freedom from demonic bondages? And if so, is it not appropriate for people with pressurized lives to experience release through God-given physiological reactions? Concern about manifestations is chaff we need to brush aside.

The Need to Shout Them Out

The next chaff spillover comes from the healing revivals of the Latter Rain Movement, a move of the Holy Spirit in the late forties and early fifties. This is the practice of screaming thunderously at demons. Maybe in the early days the drama of this practice was impressive and many people received deliverance. Demons are not deaf, however. They will exit just as effectively by the confident authority expressed in a normal tone of voice.

Evil spirits are not stupid either. They can discern when someone is yelling at them to boost his or her own confidence. Our approach to deliverance needs to be a striking departure from the stereotypes of tent evangelists. The ministry will be far more appealing and effective if deliverance ministers will forego screaming at invisible entities.

The Fear of Witchcraft Curses

A widespread chaff-ridden concept is the fear that occult practitioners might pronounce curses on active Christians, thus causing many to fear drawing attention to themselves by casting out demons. I do not doubt that such pronouncements are made by witches and the like, but I am not the least bit concerned about it. A thorough study of the story of Balaam, told in Numbers 22, has convinced me of the Christian's immunity from such attempts at cursing originating in witchcraft.

Balaam had a reputation for effective curses and blessings. Consequently, Balak, the king of the Moabites, hired Balaam to curse Israel to prevent them from overrunning his nation. Balak led Balaam to three different sites from which he directed Balaam to curse the Israelites. No matter how much Balak urged Balaam to curse them, however, he could not do so. Instead, Balaam spoke a great blessing over the nation of Israel.

When Balaam looked out over the twelve tribes of Israel camped in formation according to their numbers, do you realize what he saw? He saw what appeared to be a huge cross, with the Tabernacle of Moses in the middle of the cross section. The tribes with the greater numbers of people camped in a straight line running from east to west. The tribes with fewer numbers were lined from north to south.

The tents were covered with black badger skins, so their formation looked exactly like a huge, black cross. What Balaam looked upon, therefore, was a black cross with the flames and smoke from the burning sacrifices central in it. It was a prophetic depiction foreshadowing Jesus' sacrificial death. Here is the message: Curses stop at the cross and all who look to it for salvation will be blessed.

This is the summation of what Balaam reported to Balak: "I cannot curse those whom God has not cursed. Neither sorcery nor divination will work against Israel. I have received a commandment to bless and I cannot reverse it."

Perhaps the most startling statement by Balaam was that God had not seen any wickedness in Israel that might have opened the way for his curses to succeed. It also demonstrates the Lord's capacity to forgive and to forget past sins (see Numbers 22:6; 23:8, 19–23).

Prior to this incident involving Balak and Balaam, thousands of Jews had died in the wilderness due to rebellion. The entire house of Korah the Levite had been swallowed by the earth. Two hundred and fifty of their sympathizers had been consumed by lightning. Fourteen thousand and seven hundred people had died in a plague for complaining about the death of Korah's household. In addition, for the sin of disrespecting Moses' leadership, untold numbers were bitten by serpents and many died. (See Numbers 16:29–35, 49; 21:5–6.) By any definition, that could be considered wickedness in Israel.

Yet God chose to forgive and to forget all these incidents. His will for Israel under the Old Covenant was blessing. How much more is it God's will for the Body of Christ to prosper and to be in health under the better New Covenant? Christians have no need to worry about getting blindsided by curses from the devil's servants.

The Need for Ongoing Generational Repentance

I have counseled many Christians about their deliverance needs, and have noted how many have wrongfully come to believe that they need to renounce their familial histories again and again if they hope to experience deliverance. Thus, at the onset of deliverance ministry, they begin to cite their family sins that could have led to demonic attacks on them. This is another instance of chaff.

"My grandfather was an Indian medicine man."

"My dad was a member of the Masonic Lodge."

"My mother was a witch, and she told me I was born with psychic abilities."

In most instances, a previous minister has already led the

individual in the proper renunciations. Whenever I learn that is the case, my approach is to ask a number of questions to correct their thinking.

"Have you previously been through deliverance?"

"Yes."

"Did you specifically repent of and renounce the historical sins that you have mentioned?"

"Yes."

"Have you since engaged in any of the activities that you have renounced?"

"No, I would never do so!"

"When you were born again, how many times did you say the sinner's prayer of repentance?"

"Once."

"So, God forgave you for all of your past sins with a single prayer of repentance?"

"Yes."

"After salvation when you commit a sin, how many times do you have to ask forgiveness for that sin in order to be cleansed by the blood of Jesus?"

"Just once."

"Then why would the ancestral sins that you have already renounced and for which you have no responsibility have any bearing on you now?"

"I don't know."

The fact is that repenting of and renouncing the same generational sins over and over again is unnecessary. Furthermore, your children's children won't ever have to renounce those sins of your ancestors that you have confessed. Any possible generational curses stopped with your one-time renunciation.

The biblical truth is that you are a new creation in Christ. You no longer have any generational sins to pass down to your descendants. Your Father is God and your elder Brother is Jesus. Through redemption, your adopted family tree no longer consists of sinners. It is composed of the redeemed of the Lord of heaven and of earth. As a new creation in Christ, your DNA contains no curses to pass down.

If you have renounced the connection with family sins, you have made enough renunciations. Any current demonic issues you might have are not from generational curses.

Rejecting Signs and Wonders

I call *anointing quenchers* those folks who feel it is their calling to throw cold water on whatever new and interesting trends the Lord is sending to rekindle passion for Him and His ways. Their buckets invariably overflow with statements like, "Well, you know, the devil does that, too." Unfortunately, some Bible teachers are among the chief anointing quenchers.

Christians predisposed to negative mindsets are deeply influenced by this teaching. As a result, they also develop the tendency to label any type of spiritual phenomena they do not understand as an act of Satan. They become authorities on satanic deception, on what is "of God" and what is "not of God." They renounce as New Age almost anything that seems new. That habit of making quick judgments is risky business. It may cause a person to verge on blaspheming the Holy Spirit if the work they are criticizing is a genuine move of God.

The Lord reserves the right to perform unique and unusual feats. The Bible is filled with these incidents. The Bible also contains concepts that the Body of Christ has not yet explored. As we approach the Second Coming of Christ, we can expect increasing Scripture-based revelation. The Body of Christ needs this revelation to equip us for the challenges of the end times. I contend that even with all the teachings we have heard and understood in the Word of God, it likely contains more that we have not yet heard and understood.

Somehow the critics of unusual phenomena think that if something is given by God it will line up with human logic. That can be a significant deception. God often chooses to speak symbolically. Ezekiel's vision of a wheel in the middle of a wheel defies reasoning. The scenes John reported in the book of Revelation have yet to be fully explained. After the resurrection, Jesus walked through a wall to meet with His disciples. Why would Jesus do such a thing rather than entering conventionally or knocking on the door? There is no logical reason other than the fact that He seems to enjoy doing marvelous stuff. Jesus would have been no less the risen Savior had He come through the door.

Christians who fret about New Age contamination would likely have found the ministry of the apostle Paul disconcerting had they witnessed it. Take his acquaintance with the deeds and writings of prophets and poets who worshiped heathen deities. He called upon that knowledge when he encountered the Athenian philosophers on Areopagus, or Mars Hill. It was his way of identifying with his audience.

Hundreds of years prior to the advent of Christ, a devastating plague hit Athens. In an attempt to quench it, the civil authorities sent for the heathen poet and prophet, Epimenides of Knossos, Crete. He gave them curious instructions. A herd of sheep was to be subjected to a fast for three days. Afterward, the sheep were to be turned loose to graze on the grassy slopes of Mars Hill. Epimenides told the elders that some of those sheep would refuse to eat. Altars to the Unknown God were to be erected on the spots on which those sheep had stood, and they were then to sacrifice on those altars all the sheep that had not eaten. The very next day following the sacrifice, the plague miraculously ended.

Acts 17:22–23 relates how Paul began his sermon by making reference to their altar "To the Unknown God." He knew the supernatural history of how the altar had come into being centuries before his arrival on the scene. Divine foresight had granted a miracle to prepare the way for Paul's sermon.

Later in his message, Paul quoted a poem by Epimenides. Paul's quote is found in the first half of Acts 17:28: "For in Him we live and move and have our being." In the second half of the verse, Paul quoted Aratus: "For we are also His offspring." Aratus was a Greek poet who died in 240 B.C. The poem was *Phaenomena*. It spoke of how all mankind are the offspring of Zeus, the chief deity of the Greeks. Paul later quoted one of Epimenides' prophecies in Titus 1:12 and endorsed it as true.

Certainly, the Lord expects us to be vigilant about discerning deceptive doctrines. That does not give us, however, a mandate to dismiss every new concept we hear. We must remember that the devil hates the anointing of the Holy Spirit. He is delighted to have us labeling God's acts as his own.

I am of the opinion that many quick judgments of anointing quenchers can actually be inspired by a spirit of antichrist. The word *Christ* is defined as "the Anointed One." The prefix *anti* means "against." Jesus told His disciples that whoever rejected them was in effect rejecting Him. Those who oppose God's servants and denounce their works as satanic are in opposition to Christ. Believers should never do that. Bible teachers should be particularly cautious to have the facts right before passing judgment.

The Bible speaks of wondrous signs. The reason they are wondrous is often because they have no exact natural or biblical precedents. The Old Testament was the only authoritative source of God's Word before the New Testament was written. On the Day of Pentecost, when the 120 disciples were praying for the coming of the Holy Spirit, they suddenly had tongues of fire appear over their heads. The Old Testament does not have any references to that specific phenomenon. Yet it would have been tragic for the disciples to reject the infilling of the Holy Spirit because the Scriptures as they knew them had no mention of the appearance of flames of fire on the recipients' heads. It is important for us to resist the overtures of a spirit of antichrist, which opposes or quenches the anointing. We must not reject signs, wonders and teachings with which God intends to bless us.

Being Naturally Supernatural about Deliverance

Even with ever-present chaff to be winnowed out, believers can gather a wonderful harvest of wheat in the field of deliverance and share it with others. It is our responsibility as Christians who understand deliverance to be circumspect about the manner and timing of how we share what we have learned. I instruct those who attend my seminars to present deliverance in a relaxed fashion without any sense of sensationalism or urgency. I call it the naturally supernatural approach. It is especially appropriate when dealing with the unconverted.

I enjoy interactions with people who have not yet found faith in Christ. When conversing with them, they often make mention of circumstances that hint of demonic issues. With some of the people I encounter, the focus of the conversation is the relational problems they have battled in life. With others, the conversation focuses on their interest in occult and New Age topics. I have found it beneficial to be a good listener. After these folks have expressed themselves, I ask if it would be all right with them for me to share my experiences with the topic we are discussing. In doing so, I make every effort to avoid sensationalism.

More often than not, I tell them about my personal deliverances from evil spirits. I do not mention demons per se, as the mention of the word might tend to get the conversation off track. I simply say there was something in my personality that drove me to do this or that. I tell them that I spoke to the issue as though it were a person and told it to leave my life. Then I speak of the subsequent freedom I experienced.

If they indicate further interest, I ask if they would like for me to pray with them to bring them the same relief I have found. If they answer in the affirmative, I ask if it would be all right for me to place my hand on their backs as I pray. At that point, I address any suspected spirits as things rather than demons. Afterward, I ask them how they are feeling. The usual response is that they feel better. I then ask if I might maintain contact with them. Once the trust factor is firmly established in whatever relationship develops from that point, at the appropriate time I explain further what happened to them.

I usually begin at that point with a comment about the existence of airborne germs and bacteria that are invisible to the naked eye. From there, I quote passages indicating that we face invisible foes in the atmosphere around us. I describe rationally what demons are and how they function. I add that we do not need to fear them as we have been immunized against them by God's saving grace. I further explain how to deal with a spirit that somehow slips through our defenses. At the end of the conversation, I always present the plan of salvation.

With people who have dabbled in the occult, I always ask them what they are searching for. Inevitably, what they are seeking is something attainable through salvation and the legitimate gifts of the Holy Spirit. I tell them about the gifts of the Spirit and the benefits I have experienced. I then ask them if any unusual problems have evolved in their lives during their occult searches. Many describe curses that are often attached to occult exploration. I then pray for them in the same way I described above, with the follow-up procedures that I previously outlined.

The citizens of our society are looking for life, not religiosity. Jesus did not die on the cross to institute a superstitious "step-on-a-crack-and-the-boogieman-is-going-to-get-you" religion. Our goal should always be to persuade people of the simplicity of life in Christ Jesus. I believe that comes as we attempt to be supernaturally natural in our attempts to winnow out chaff from the wheat in ministry.

In the next chapter, we will examine additional avenues of deliverance—freedom that can take place through the sacraments and other Christian practices. Holy Communion, water baptism, the laying on of hands and prayer cloths can all be effective tools for deliverance. When properly understood, those practices are transformed from traditional rituals into life-giving acts of faith.

12

Deliverance in Conjunction with Other Biblical Practices

Scripture ordains a number of practices for the Body of Christ, including the sacraments. These practices were never intended to be observed as empty rituals of a bygone era. When properly understood, biblical practices can be dynamic tools of deliverance. This chapter will discuss four particular practices: Holy Communion, water baptism, laying on of hands and the use of prayer cloths.

The Lord's Supper

Christ is our Passover Lamb. A liturgical synonym for Holy Communion is the Paschal (Passover) Meal. The first Passover was observed by the Jews on the eve of their miraculously rapid departure from Egypt. Some authorities estimate that there were as many as three million participants in that exodus. The Bible tells us in Psalm 105:37 that there were no sick among them when they left. How and when they got healed holds an important lesson for all of us who are interested in healing and deliverance.

Healing and deliverance from evil spirits is made available to believers on the basis of the New Covenant in Jesus' body and blood. The first Passover meal of the Israelites typified the future celebration of the Lord's Supper. The Jews were most likely suffering from all kinds of ailments and maladies—whether diverse diseases commonly found in Egypt, birth defects, the ill effects of old age, injuries building Egyptian monuments. Whatever the problem, these persons could well have been healed as they were partaking of the Passover meal.

On the deliverance side, that Passover meal may well have driven out numerous evil spirits from the Jews. Two major types would have been spirits of infirmity that carried many of the sicknesses of Egypt, and emotion-influencing demons that gained entrance through the stresses of slavery. It is my conviction that the Paschal meal brought about both healing and deliverance for God's people, and I believe Communion in our times carries the same blessed qualities many times over.

Whenever I conduct a Communion service, I urge people to believe God for miracles of healing and deliverance from bondages. The following report from a Cuban pastor who is an associate of mine is an example of what can happen during the Lord's Supper to deliver people of evil spirits.

My friend of many years, Seby Matacena, invited me to hold a deliverance seminar at his church in Miami, Florida. In Seby's church was a young Nicaraguan couple who were in training for ministry. The young woman's father detested Seby and his church. He would often blaspheme them with terrible denouncements. One night, the father showed up at the church with a look of defiance. Little did he know that he was to have a surprising appointment with God.

In the course of the service that evening, Seby spontaneously decided to serve the Lord's Supper. To everyone's shock, the father came forward to receive it. As he swallowed the bread, it lodged in his throat and he began to choke. He fell to the floor and turned blue. Someone tried the Heimlich maneuver on him, but to no avail. The man passed out from asphyxiation, and a frantic call was made to the paramedics. But while the paramedics were on their way to the church, the father suddenly recovered, stood up and began to hug Seby and the couple.

"I was choking to death," he explained. "Jesus appeared to me. He told me that I would surely die on the spot if I did not repent and renounce my blaspheming against Seby and the church. I did exactly as the Lord commanded and the bread passed into my stomach."

All of the people involved in that church know that the father was delivered of a hostile spirit that despised the anointing of Jesus Christ on God's servants. In light of this story, I urge you to look upon Communion as a vital portion of the children's bread of deliverance. Bear that fact in mind whenever you are a recipient of the Lord's Supper. Exercise your faith that any stubborn sicknesses or latent evil spirits may well depart from you as you partake of this holy sacrament.

Water Baptism

From earliest times in the Church, adults who were baptized renounced Satan and all of his works prior to their immersions. The Roman Catholic Church and some Protestant denominations have a similar confession for those who were baptized as infants and are receiving confirmation into the Church, as well as for those re-affirming their baptisms. Deliverance as part of this sacrament is a powerful means of liberation.

Some years ago I took part in a ministry conference in Baltimore, Maryland, in which it was my responsibility to concentrate my efforts on casting out demons from those who were considered "difficult cases."

During the conference, a middle-aged man and his wife came to me for help. The husband was suffering from erectile dysfunction problems for which there were no medical explanations. The couple said the Lord had revealed to them that the source of the problem was demonic.

One of the first questions I asked the husband was whether or not he had a complete understanding of the full purpose of baptism. He admitted he did not, as he had been baptized as an infant by his parents in a mainline denomination. His parents' understanding of baptism was merely ceremonial and lacked a full understanding of the impact of the baptismal vows they were making for him.

I asked him directly, "Are you willing to undergo water baptism by immersion as a means of deliverance?"

"Yes," the husband replied.

"I am going to fill up a bathtub here in the hotel and immerse you in it. You are a tall man and the bathtub is short. I'll immerse your upper torso and head first, then immerse your lower body. It will be reminiscent of your denomination's baptism, but you are going to get a lot wetter. I'll lay you down in the name of the Father, the Son and the Holy Spirit. Then I will command the troubling demon to leave you just before immersing your lower half. Do you both agree to this remedy?"

Both husband and wife nodded in agreement, and I proceeded to baptize the man in the manner that I had described. Nothing perceptible took place for them, but we all knew that he had obeyed the Lord's directive for him for deliverance.

The following morning the couple greeted me in the lobby of the hotel with huge grins and a mutual gesture of thumbs-up. Apparently the baptism had been the missing factor in the man's healing, and the problem had been taken care of.

At that same conference, I met a United States army colonel who flew in from the base where he was stationed in Germany to seek deliverance. The officer was of Lutheran background, and he told me that he had suffered from deep depression all of his life. He had been married twice and was about to enter a third marriage.

When he heard about deliverance, he became convinced that it was what he needed in order to be set free before the depression had a chance to ruin his current relationship. I chose to minister deliverance to him in the waters of baptism.

I explained that the impending doom the Israelites felt from the pursuit of Pharaoh's wicked forces ended when those Egyptians were drowned in the Red Sea. I proclaimed that it would be the same with his depression. This time, the plan was to baptize him in the hotel's indoor swimming pool.

As we were about to enter the pool, I explained to the officer: "Baptism is a burial of your old man, and it can be viewed as your separation from any attached evil spirits. Your baptism will leave all depression behind, buried in the waters of baptism."

The colonel followed me into the pool, and just before I submersed him, I issued this order: "I command the spirit of gloomy darkness to leave you in the name of Jesus of Nazareth." Then I leaned him back into the waters of the pool and baptized him.

After getting out of the water, he kept staring back into the pool. The next day he came to meet me for a follow-up session.

"How are you doing?" I asked him.

"I've never felt better in my life," the officer replied.

"Do you have any need of deliverance from any other problems that might be demonic?" I inquired further.

"I'm all clear, Jim," the colonel stated. "Yesterday after my baptism, I looked back into the swimming pool and saw the old me floating there, face-down like a bloated corpse. I'm a new creation in Christ Jesus. Any evil spirits that I hosted have been through the pool's filtering system several times by now. They most definitely are not in me."

As I have mentioned, I believe that a huge revival is on the way. As people stream into the Kingdom of God in response to the moving of the Holy Spirit in the days ahead, hundreds of thousands will be baptized. I am thoroughly convinced that if pastors could come to unity about the effectual purposes of water baptism in relation to deliverance, the need for personal deliverances would be greatly diminished. If we could approach baptism as this colonel did, the demons inhabiting many would be left in the waters of baptism, commanded and compelled to leave their hosts.

Laying On of Hands

Laying hands on people is one of six foundational doctrines of Christianity noted in Hebrews 6:1–3. Jesus laid His hands on the sick and the demonized to bring about cures. The disciples laid hands on people to transmit blessings and spiritual gifts. This legacy has been passed to us.

I sometimes choose to lay my hands on people as a means of quieting various types of aggravating spirits at work in them. It is effective with believers and unbelievers alike. I do so in an informal way without announcing what I am doing. With a contentious person, I put forth my right hand to shake his and grasp his elbow with my left hand. Verbally I say something cordial. Inwardly, I am binding the hostile spirit and commanding it to be silent. I have silenced more than a few argumentative demons in that manner. It is certainly better than allowing tempers to get out of hand.

I also look for appropriate opportunities to pick up whiny and fearful children. While holding my hands to their backs, I come against whatever spirits I believe might be troubling them. The tactic has earned me a reputation for being exceptionally good with kids.

Some people have expressed concern about laying hands on someone in a deliverance situation, fearing that it might be possible for evil spirits to transfer from the individual to them in the process. I do not believe that this is anything we need to worry about. Remember that Jesus laid His hands on the woman with a crippling spirit.

Evil spirits regard their hosts as their homes. Malicious powers do not welcome transfers from one domicile to another; usually they must be evicted forcefully. We can have every assurance that the blood of the Lamb is capable of protecting a believer who is engaged in prayers of blessings or deliverance.

Part of the misperception about this comes from those who use 1 Timothy 5:22 as a proof text for the possibility of picking up an evil spirit by laying hands on someone in deliverance. The verse says: "Do not lay hands on anyone hastily, nor share in other people's sins."

I do not believe this verse is making reference to the transference of demons. The wording pertains to laying hands on people too hastily in ordaining them to spiritual ministry. The implication is that officials are responsible for the conduct of those whom they endorse by the laying on of hands. The New Living Translation gives a helpful rendering of 1 Timothy 5:22 in this regard: "Never be in a hurry about appointing an elder. Do not participate in the sins of others. Keep yourself pure."

We see quite clearly in the life of Jesus that the laying on of hands can be a powerful tool in the healing and deliverance process. In addition, it is a wonderful tool in the process of imparting blessing and gifting to people who are being set free to serve the Lord.

Prayer Cloths

The practice of sending anointed prayer cloths has raised more than one eyebrow over the years as it has been reduced to a means for fund-raising. That use does not fall within scriptural parameters. The originator of the practice of sending prayer cloths was the apostle Paul. He did so because he was exceptionally busy during his two years of ministry at Ephesus.

Throughout Asia Minor people were getting saved, healed and delivered of evil spirits. Paul could not travel to every location that needed the resident power of the Holy Spirit that flowed through him.

Handkerchiefs that he had touched and aprons he had worn were sent to the sick and to the demonized who were not able to travel to him. Scripture attests in Acts 19:11–12 that "unusual miracles" were brought about by the practice. Those who were physically ill were restored to health, and demons fled from those who came into contact with these pieces of cloth. The implication of his actions is that the anointing of the Holy Spirit has tangibility: It can be transferred to and through inanimate objects.

Early in my ministry, I found it beneficial for items that I had prayed over to be sent to those who were sick and tormented by demons. I call it God's secret weapon of deliverance. Here is why.

There are occasions when people ask me to help relatives who are resistant to spiritual matters. I ask them to bring me a favorite item of clothing that the person wears or to purchase an article they would wear. I place the item under me as I sleep. (The pieces Paul sent were most likely from his leather work aprons. I think that it was the fabric's long-term exposure to his body's sweat and oils that brought on the deposits of the anointing. Sleeping on articles is a close representation of what happened in Acts.)

When I lie down to sleep, I bind the spirits that are suspected of inhabiting the person. Then when I return the cloth to the concerned relatives, I instruct them to give the cloth items to the afflicted without saying anything about what has transpired. I tell them to watch patiently and see what the Lord does. I have received many reports of complete reversals of attitude and behavior in the lives of the recipients.

A Presbyterian clergyman had a parishioner whose teenage son had been institutionalized with a religious fixation: The young man claimed to be Jesus. To approach him about deliverance would have only made matters worse. The pastor brought me a T-shirt that the teen liked. I prayed over it, slept on it and returned it to the pastor, who then gave the shirt back to the boy's mother. The day after the boy got the shirt back and started wearing it in the mental institution, the teen was discharged. The pastor told me the young man had been completely restored to his right mind.

The daughter and son-in-law of an excessively manipulative woman came to Derek Prince for help. He instructed them to get an article of her clothing and pray over it, binding the spirits of witchcraft that operated in the woman. After they had prayed, the daughter took the item to her mother, who happened to be washing clothes at the time. The mother grabbed the article and threw it directly into the washer.

The daughter later admitted to Derek that her heart sank when her mother tossed the garment into the washer. She incorrectly assumed the anointing would be "washed away." But just a little while later, she had the opportunity to testify to God's greatness. As it turned out, there was not even a need for the woman to wear the garment. Simply touching it as she put the item in the wash was enough to subdue the spirits of witchcraft. Shortly after throwing the item into the washer, the manipulative behavior of the mother ceased. The couple said that her behavior had become entirely amiable and agreeable.

PART THREE

Deeper into Deliverance

This part offers advanced techniques, bringing light to areas of deliverance that often escape attention. We will begin with the important area of pulling down behavior-influencing strongholds in our memories. Then we will learn to discern whether or not we are living under the consequences of breaking a vow; Jesus said that we should not make vows and yet many of us utter them in our daily conversations. Next we will delve into the manipulative influences of soul ties with bygone loves and current control freaks.

In chapters that follow we will see why discomforts about certain sexual practices are nudges from God. We will look at a new approach to banish chronic physical pains. We will definitely find a way to brighten the atmosphere of our homes.

Most importantly we will be given the assurance that we are well equipped to meet and to conquer whatever the enemy dishes out. No one of any generation is better suited for what is coming down the pike than this one. According to Psalm 139:16, God recorded the days of our lives in His book before we physically existed.

The deliverance methods that we discover in Part 3 will equip us to face the most difficult scenarios. Remember: We were created to triumph.

13

Obliterating Demonic Strongholds in Your Mind

The insights in this chapter came to me in bits and pieces over a period of more than thirty years. The method I describe has been distilled from a mixture of my own insights, ministry experience and observation of other valid ministries. In this chapter, we will focus on pulling down demonic strongholds in our minds that have come out of painful memories. Through this ministry, we can more easily cultivate the mind of Christ and come into freedom from demonic torment (see 1 Corinthians 2:16; 2 Corinthians 10:4–5).

Over the years, much helpful teaching has emerged on the topic of pulling down mental strongholds set against the knowledge of God. Believers have been encouraged to attack citadels of misinformation in their minds through the spiritual disciplines of prayer, Bible study and by purposely replacing worldly perspectives with biblical perspectives. Those pursuits are tested and true and a vital part of the Christian life.

The application I describe in this chapter, however, employs a power stronger than the disciplines of man. In addition, this mode of deliverance predates all those other forms. It replicates the ministry of Jesus as seen in the biblical record where people were set free merely by Jesus speaking His Word.

During His earthly sojourn, Jesus spoke from without—that is, He employed each individual's physical sense of hearing. In this model of ministry, He speaks from within. The results are the same. This method is distinctive in that the on-site minister is Jesus Christ Himself. At the invitation of the victimized seeker, the Risen Lord speaks words of deliverance from within, obliterating the grip that painful memories have on our minds.

Satan's Armor

In Luke 11:20–26, Jesus spoke about deliverance and the process by which demons leave the person they are troubling. We learn from this passage that one of the reasons an evil spirit is forced to vacate its host is because the armor in which the demon trusted has been taken away. Jesus ripped away the trusted armor of demons by His gentle but authoritative words. And what is that armor? Often it is the stronghold Satan has established in a person's memories connected with the events of life.

Demons frame their strongholds around memories of incidents where a person may be at fault, or those incidents where others wittingly or unwittingly perpetrated some kind of injury upon that person. In those cases, the devil, who is the father of lies, implants deceitful misinformation that maligns God and depicts the person himself as inept and unreliable.

Spiritual warfare is much like natural warfare. In actual warfare, enemy agents often infiltrate centers of influence in a nation targeted for takeover. They circulate various forms of misinformation within the society that is designed to discourage and to intimidate. That misinformation leaves its victims in a vulnerable condition, saddled with fear or insecurity.

Satan's demons do much the same with us when they create

strongholds in our memories. Many of our negative emotional reactions are the result of deceptive misinformation planted in our personalities during our formative years by injurious experiences. Our adverse reactions as adults often spring from strongholds of misinformation implanted in childhood.

Satan uses demonic forces to goad young, innocent minds to interpret injurious events as their own fault. In doing so, demons establish strongholds that will ensure future difficulties. The deceptive programming in our cognitive processes makes us feel hopelessness, shame and guilt about our repeated sins. In addition, the misinformation twists our perceptions about the nature of God. We envision Him as a bully looking for opportunities to scold and punish us for our sins. The outcome of such misinformation, and the strongholds it forms, is that many believers treat the Lord more or less like a dentist: They avoid contact out of fear of what He might say and do.

All the while, Jesus Christ is available within. He is far kinder than performance-centered religion and demons would lead us to believe. In fact, if we simply ask Him, He is prepared to intervene in our lives with mercy and tenderness, rather than with the wrath and judgment we wrongly attribute to Him.

The Voice

When Jesus speaks into a stronghold, all misinformation is dispelled. Every syllable of every word of His voice from within has power that resonates in the believer and produces satisfaction, instant peace and resolution of inner conflicts.

In the following pages, I give you two personal ministry experiences where the voice of the Lord shattered strongholds in my mind and demons fled. In the first scenario the details about how and when the demon established the stronghold were irrelevant to my deliverance. I called on the Lord, asking Him to speak into the matter. I was candid with the Lord about what I really felt and thought. It included the confession of my fear of what God might say about my sins.

The second ministry experience employed a mode of pulling down strongholds that requires detailed information. It might sound a little like the healing of the memories, but it is not. Memories of events are not eradicated or changed. Current emotions are used to trace back to memories where demonic forces established strongholds. The Lord's voice, spoken into the situation, destroys the stronghold, but the memory remains intact. I will show how I used this "back-tracking" technique in a conference ministry time, and then help you employ it yourself.

A Nasty Distraction

From 1978 to 1983 I served as what might best be described as an overseer of a global nondenominational network of churches. The constant travel and ministering to congregations required for this position was easy for me. The function that I found difficult was working through interpreters when counseling pastors about everything from troubled marriages to church squabbles. I earnestly wanted to help them, but often felt that I was not as successful as I could have been had we not had a language barrier.

My reaction was frustrated anger. Frustration seemed to seethe beneath the surface of my emotions all of the time during those years. I constantly had to suppress inclinations to lash out at people. I managed to maintain a pleasant tone of voice and a ready smile when in public. Around my home and office, however, when I was not directly engaged in conversation, I let down my guard. My expression darkened into a scowl.

My office crew began to call it "the face." I did not like the idea of people tiptoeing around me for fear that the emotions behind "the face" might suddenly explode. But that prospect, rather than helping to temper my emotions, only increased my agitation and led me to do something I thought I would never do: I began to use tobacco. I did not smoke it, as the smell of smoke would have been too risky for my reputation. I chewed it. It was a messy, disgusting business. Somehow the misinformation that got programmed into my psyche was that my use of tobacco was a suitable escape valve to prevent the frustration that would cause me to exhibit "the face." It did nothing of the kind.

I never got hooked on the stuff, but chewed often enough to be scandalized by my own behavior. After each use I would repent and throw away the unused portion, only to find myself buying another bagful a month or so later. Then I slipped into the miserable offender pattern, plagued by guilt and shame at my nasty indulgence.

I was sure that if God ever spoke to me about the matter, it would be a flaming indictment. I feared judgment from Him in the form of the loss of my ministry. With these ongoing frustrations and guilt taking a substantial toll on my peace of mind, I decided to take a month off to find relief.

Run Hard, Put Away Wet

During my month off, I decided to go to the Benedictine Monastery in Pecos, New Mexico. The monks there were charismatic by experience and ecumenically disposed. One day during that time, while meditating in one of the prayer rooms, I gathered the courage to ask the Lord to speak to me. He did so with a symbolic vision that relieved and revitalized me, and it was far from the scorching indictment I had expected to receive from Him.

In the vision, I saw an Arabian horse that was sweaty and streaked with saliva all along its neck. Its head hung low as though it was too heavy to lift. As the expression goes, the horse had been "run hard and put away wet." Horses left in that condition are subject to pneumonia and paralysis.

Next in the vision, a distinguished-looking trainer entered the scene and placed a training halter and lead on the horse. He led it to a stable where he bathed it and brushed it down. The horse's deep red coat began to glisten. Its mane and tail, freshly washed, showed a gorgeous strawberry-blond color. Suddenly, it dawned on me. That Arabian steed was me, and the Trainer was the Lord.

The Trainer then saddled the horse with a western saddle. When

He mounted the horse, its nostrils flared and its head perked up with excitement. The Trainer then worked the horse around the ring and, after putting the horse through its paces, reined it to a stop. The Trainer leaned forward, patted the steed and affectionately hugged its neck. Then He whispered into the horse's ear, "I appreciate you."

When I heard those words from the Trainer in the vision, spoken to that horse that I identified as myself, I sobbed with joy and slipped to my knees in worship. At that moment, the constant sense of frustration ended. From that moment on, "the face" disappeared, as did my need for chewing tobacco. The deliverance was accomplished without my ever needing to utter a single command for a demon to leave me.

Roots Revealed

Years later I revisited the Arabian horse vision and was thanking God for what it had done in my life. I asked Him about the origins of my frustrations leading to tobacco use. He reminded me of an incident when I was eight years old. I was spending a weekend with my grandparents. While wandering around their neighborhood on Friday afternoon, I spotted two boys of my age smoking. I reported it with no little indignation to my grandfather, who was a smoker. His response was covert and mischievous.

The following day was Saturday, and he and my grandmother had to go to work. Before Granddaddy left, he tore a cigarette in half. He placed one half in the den ashtray, and the other half in the living room ashtray. I resisted the temptation until about noon. I gave in, lit up and coughed my way through both halves of the cigarette.

That evening after supper, Granddaddy called me into the den. He had both ashtrays in his hands, with the butts of the halves I had smoked glaring at me. "I suppose those naughty boys that you saw smoking broke into the house and smoked these?"

It frustrated me to no end that I had been so easily set up and busted. Apparently, it was that incident that the devil used to create a stronghold within me interlinking tobacco with frustration. The blessed news is that God intervened by giving me the Arabian horse vision. Regardless of my sullenness and my nasty periodic tobacco blunders, the Lord told me that He appreciated me. What a gift! What a liberating God!

Words of Liberation

The second ministry example where the voice of the Lord shattered strongholds came from a time my pastor friend Seby Matacena, whom I mentioned in the last chapter, invited me to hold a deliverance seminar at his church. Seby is well versed in deliverance. During our pre-seminar discussions, I asked him to update me on how he was ministering deliverance in personal counseling sessions.

"You know, Jim, though Jesus promised that He would speak to His sheep and lead them by His voice, most have never heard the voice of the Lord. Many are afraid of what they might hear, especially those entangled with habitual sin issues. Though they genuinely love the Lord, they keep Him at a reverential distance.

"Now, of course they need deliverance," he continued. "The question is what mode is most suitable for each individual. At times, it is right for deliverance ministers to battle demons into submission with spiritual warfare Scriptures. At other times, nothing will do as well as Jesus' voice speaking words of liberation to a captive."

He went on to state his belief that much of the preaching today conditions people to anticipate that God's comments about their sins will be harsh and condemning. His solution was to begin each deliverance session by counseling the people about God's love for them.

"I want them to know that God enjoys His kids even when they are going down the mistake-filled road to maturity. Encouragement about God's love paves the way for them to want to hear from the Lord. It also helps them recognize the Lord's cheerful, comforting words that they might normally brush aside as wishful thinking.

"Once the love factor soaks in," he said, "I ask them for the details about why they made the appointment. From there, I encourage the person to ask the Lord to speak to them about His perception of the situation they are faced with. Regularly, the Lord speaks tailor-made words of comfort and affirmation. The Lord's voice within the person's soul knocks the condemning supports out from under the demons. The resident evil spirits normally leave without a fuss."

I asked him to give me an example of what he might say to convince people of God's affection. He replied by speaking to me as he would a counselee.

"Do you know that God chose you to be His child and appointed you for a high calling of good works before time began? That's right! You were discussed by name in the divine council of the Godhead. The Father, the Son and the Holy Spirit, according to their infinite wisdom and foresight, saw you as strategic for this generation.

"God knows the end from the beginning. No matter what you've done following your conversion, you haven't shocked or scandalized the Lord. If today were your adoption day, Father God would pick you for adoption just as He did when you were saved years ago. That's why there was such joy in the presence of God when you were born again. Just like the scene in the musical *Little Orphan Annie*, when everyone was rejoicing about Annie's adoption, the host of heaven was gleefully shouting, 'We got Jim! Jim's in the Kingdom. We got Jim!' There has never been a day that God was not happy to see you at His throne of grace. Now, what problem brought you to me today?"

This approach resonated with me. All that my colleague had shared matched my own growing understanding of pulling down strongholds of misinformation. I told Seby about an experience I had had in prayer in which the Lord helped me understand why, years before, I usually responded to situations that required patience with anything but. Traffic jams, for instance, that threatened to make me late for an appointment could set off volleys of profanity.

After one such incident, I followed that feeling of impatience all the way back to an experience I had had as a toddler. I was standing in a driveway with my back to a partially open garage door. Both the driveway and the door were painted white, and the slight opening of the door revealed a dark and scary interior. I was gripping my diaper like a guardrail for fear that I would fall backward into what looked to me like the yawning blackness of oblivion. I was crying and screaming for help. No one in the family tried to rescue me. They just laughed and, amazingly, got a camera and took photographs.

I asked the Lord to give me His take on what had happened. Instantaneously, I got an answer. As I heard His words of explanation within the inner man of my spirit, I felt something evil loosening its grip in my heart and my mind. I believe it was a demon of impatience. At that moment, I sensed the Good Shepherd was saying, *I didn't orchestrate the happenings of your formative years. What the enemy meant for evil, I have turned around for good. Throughout your life and ministry you have been sensitive to others. You've done all within your power to respond to people in a manner affirming their worth and their relevance to Me. I commend you for your faithfulness.*

I told Seby that ever since the time that stronghold was toppled by the Lord's voice, I had not had a single episode of impatient fuming and cursing.

Seby and I agreed that for the conference's deliverance session, he would begin by speaking about the love of God. Then I would address the issue of how demonic strongholds are rooted in our memories, and walk the attendees through the deliverance process.

"Backtracking" Emotions

During the conference in which Seby and I were ministering, as time came for the actual deliverance, I used the technique the Lord had shown me, and which I call "backtracking," to help people identify the misinformation strongholds that need to be obliterated. I helped them backtrack current disruptive emotions to earlier events they held in their memories where strongholds had been established. Here is the way the ministry unfolded.

"I would like for those who sense they have demonic issues, and who want help, to stand," I said, as I began the time of ministry. Approximately thirty people stood to their feet.

"Now I invite you to identify the negative emotion that

accompanied the last incident you had where a suspected demon caused you problems. Once you have recalled the event and have identified the negative emotion you experienced, please raise your hand." Most everyone responded.

"The next step is for you to try to recall the earliest life incident where you felt that same intensity of the negative emotion. That is likely the place that a demonic spirit established a stronghold of misinformation in your psyche. When you've located the memory, raise your hand."

Now, it could be that if an incident happened to us early in infancy, we would not be able to recall it. In that case, our spirits are smarter and more mature than our brains. Scientists are making headway in proving even prenatal awareness of external events. I have cast spirits of the fear of death from habitually whiny babies whose mothers gave strong considerations to abortion. The incessant crying stops. We can be assured that the Holy Spirit will bring to our awareness whatever will help us receive healing.

"Examine that memory for any misinformation," I continued. "It will be whatever you think about yourself that is not in agreement with what God's Word says about you—anything that is contrary to that which makes you feel good about being you. When you identify it, raise your hand.

"Now ask the Lord to speak directly to you, giving His perspective about the incident and the misinformation that was planted with it. Raise your hand to signal you have heard from the Lord. Those who want to come up to share what they experience and who want to receive personal ministry may do so."

Becky's Testimony

After a few minutes, at least half of the people volunteered to come up, ranging in age from young teens to an 86-year-old woman. The results of that time of ministry were wonderful. To illustrate, I will relate one woman's story. Becky was in her early thirties and the mother of three children.

"Becky, what was the nature of your emotion?"

"It was rage and self-hatred. It has been in me for years. I've vented on everyone in my circle of relationships. I loathed my unpredictable personality."

"What was your earliest memory of those emotions and what stronghold of misinformation was established in you?"

"My father used to sexually abuse me. It made me feel so dirty. He and my mother divorced and I did not see him for years. My mother later died and during my teen years, I got pregnant out of wedlock. When my daughter was three years old, I decided to look for my father. I really needed for someone who was family to see how well my child and I were doing. I located my dad in another state. When he saw my daughter and me at his door, and I told him who we were, he did not invite us into his home. He yelled at us to leave and said he didn't ever want to see us again."

"Becky, what did Jesus say to you about all of that?"

"He told me that I was in His family, and that both He and His Dad were really proud of me."

"How do you feel now? Do you feel any of that old self-hatred and rage?"

"It is all gone. Suddenly, I really like me. I truly feel that I'm somebody who is cherished by the best of families."

Hearing Becky's testimony, I was nearly overcome by grateful emotion myself. It became apparent that the anointing to break strongholds of self-hate and anger as in Becky's experience was available to everyone there. I turned to the congregation and asked for all those who had issues with anger and self-hate to stand if they wanted liberty. Several did so and I commanded those evil spirits to leave them.

Many who resonated with her testimony and God's voice to her were also liberated. The Lord's voice had toppled the strongholds of misinformation in them. The demons had lost the deceitful armor that had previously secured their place in their hosts, and they vacated the properties.

Self-Deliverance from Strongholds

If you sense there are misinformation strongholds in your memories, you can likely deal with them in self-deliverance in the same way just described. From the testimonies provided here, use either model of hearing the voice of the Lord that seems best for you. Please begin by building yourself up with confident affirmations of the love of God. Also remember that the essential factor in destroying strongholds is the voice of the Lord. His words spoken into your darkness will dismantle the strongholds of demonic misinformation.

Specify to the Lord how the misinformation you are identifying makes you feel. Then ask Him to speak to you about it. The voice of Jesus Christ within you will specifically address and dispel the lies the enemy has planted, providing His perspective in place of the enemy's distortions.

Be patient while listening for His voice. Do not readily accept familiar religious clichés or verses you have memorized as the Lord's voice to you. They will not satisfy your soul or give lasting liberation. Authentic words from the Lord will harmonize with the Bible, but will be specifically fashioned as a direct message to you.

If what you hear sounds like a rehash of the condemnation you have already experienced, the voice is likely that of a mimicking evil spirit. Do not panic. Just "switch to another station"—the Lord's authentic voice speaking to you. The Lord has promised to guide His sheep by His voice. It will emerge in your normal cognitive processes by a distinctive mental picture, a specific phrase or a clear sensation.

There are times when people listen so intensely that their spiritual systems shut down. If you do not hear anything within about twenty minutes, stop the process. I can almost guarantee the Lord will speak to you at a later time, maybe even when you are preoccupied with other pursuits. The Holy Spirit has multitasking capability and so does your inner spirit. I have heard of numerous people who were delivered outside of the context of a ministry setting. Trust God by cooperating with His method and timing.

A Process of Sanctification

At various times in my life, I have pondered the question of why I have experienced so many deliverances. The Lord told me that it is a matter of ongoing sanctification with me. The biblical process known as sanctification can be defined as becoming experientially holy in word and deed (see 1 Peter 1:15). I take comfort in the comments of the apostle Paul in 2 Corinthians 1:8–10, when he spoke of a period of extreme pressures. His words imply that a person can have past, present and future episodes of deliverance by trusting in God "who delivered us from so great a death, and does deliver us; in whom we trust that He will still deliver us" (verse 10).

I want to encourage anyone who wrestles with the same question I have faced about multiple deliverances. It is not that we necessarily have more struggles than other people. It is just that more of our problems have demonic roots. Jesus is using deliverance as part of our sanctification process to cleanse us of every spot and wrinkle.

We should be content to flow with the uniqueness that the Creator has allotted to us. Whatever frequencies of deliverance might be appropriate for us are designed to give us a better life both now and in the age to come.

Now we turn to denouncements and vows. Few people go untouched by the power of words spoken in this manner. Whether someone rails against us or we use words to our own harm, we can be set free from the power of these spoken curses by the means of deliverance.

14

Dealing with
Denouncements and Vows

The matter of denouncements is a somewhat slippery one to get a handle on. Quite often, negative statements we make about ourselves or that others make about us are detrimental to our lives, but there is no hard and fast formula for determining when they will affect us and when they will not. Vows are equally challenging. Godly vows that we fail to keep, and flippant vows that we never should have made, can also be hazardous—but they might not be. Love covers a multitude of sins, and God does not permit reprisals in every case.

Still, many, many people suffer the effects of denouncements and vows—which are forms of curses. In cases where this does happen, curses are crucial to the topic of deliverance because demons often attach to them and intensify their detrimental effects. The curses attached to these denouncements and vows can influence finances, productivity, interpersonal relationships, children, physical health and emotional stability. If left unattended, they can go to seed within a person's life and can replicate their miserable crops throughout a lifetime. Prudence and I both needed deliverance from childhood denouncements from other people—intentional or not—that opened doors to demonic influence.

To prevent demons from continuing to grow their evil fruit, divine "crop failure" interventions are needed. The cross of Christ cancels curses attached to denouncements and vows. The blood of Jesus is the active ingredient that serves as God's "defoliate" to bring about merciful ending to the pain. I will explain how we ought to apply the blessed herbicide at the end of this chapter, including a pattern prayer that you should find helpful.

Denouncements Spoken by Another Person

Verbal denouncements are statements of condemnation spoken against a person's life, character or actions by a recognized authority figure such as a parent, a guardian, a spiritual leader—sometimes even a closely bonded boss. Verbal denouncements spoken by others, when internalized, carry great weight.

Parent/child relationships are the most common arena in which denouncements take place. Children are particularly susceptible to believing that what the authority figure says is true. Some parents fully intend to inflict harm on their children. But even parents who are usually positive and mean no harm to their children can speak rash statements that inflict damage without anyone realizing what is happening.

If these hurtful words are allowed to take root, the effects can become evident all the way into adulthood. In the paragraphs that follow, I provide an example of how a parental denouncement evolved into demon-incited destruction in a man's life. This story also speaks of how mutual forgiveness and a parent's withdrawing the harsh words bring about a welcome "crop failure."

When Luke was in his early forties, he became seriously ill. The symptoms he experienced were much like those of a heart attack: shortness of breath, pain in his chest, pain down his left arm. On numerous occasions, he was rushed to emergency rooms due to these symptoms. Each time, his heart checked out fine and the physicians were unable to identify the source of the problem. His doctor suggested the condition was psychosomatic, existing only in his head. Because Luke had a relationship with the Lord, he sought healing from reputable ministers of faith. But every attempt toward healing and relief was to no avail.

As the symptoms continued, Luke also began to have panic attacks in which the fear of impending death would paralyze him. He was so terrified, he could not bear being out of earshot of his wife. Their home was large and she frequently ran its distance to comfort him. As a Christian, he knew that heaven was his eternal destiny. But try as he might, he could not understand why he was acting like a hellbound coward. His failure caused him tremendous guilt and shame.

An endoscope exam revealed that he was suffering from acute gastritis. Luke was relieved that he did not have a heart condition, but the panic attacks and fear of death did not subside. Nor did the symptoms.

One time, as Luke was praying about his dismal situation, the Lord reminded him of an incident with his mother that had occurred in his teens. She was subject to fits of frenzied anger, and she was also prone to shouting rebukes at any family member who crossed her.

As he recalled this incident, Luke remembered that his mother had asked him to retrieve her silver punch cups that a neighbor had borrowed. On the walk home, he accidentally dropped one of the cups on the gravel road, putting some small dents in it. When Luke arrived at home, his mother spotted the dents immediately. She went ballistic.

"I hate you, Luke!" she screamed. "I wish you had been born dead."

The more Luke apologized, the more intense her rage became. At that moment, he was not aware that he was internalizing her awful denouncements. As with other such occasions, Luke had borne the flagrant curses in sullen silence. By bearing the brunt of her words without responding, Luke had mistakenly assumed that he was making himself immune to any wounds. Little did he realize that his mother's repeated outbursts were taking a cumulative toll on his emotions. And that day, when she declared that she wished he had been born dead, the demon of the fear of death had entered him.

Luke related this to me when he came to me for help, and my first advice to him was to pay his mother a visit and explain the outcome of her words. He agreed to do so.

As he sat with his mother, Luke explained his terrible plight and requested that she recant concerning her denouncements. She apologized profusely to Luke and asked him for his forgiveness. He gave it freely and embraced her. Next, Luke asked his mom to lay her hands on his head and speak a blessing over his life. She gladly did so.

Luke later testified of a tangible feeling of the fear of impending death moving out from his head as his mother blessed him. Within a week, all symptoms of gastritis and heart attack had vanished. From that day onward, Luke never experienced another panic attack of any sort.

Breaking Godly Vows

Any time we take a biblical vow, and then fail to keep it, we open ourselves to demonic affliction. We will look here at two in particular—baptismal vows and marriage vows. People make these godly vows and swear in the presence of both God and man that they will keep them. Even a conservative estimate of the number of people who are suffering the consequences of failing to take those oaths seriously is frightening.

Baptismal Vows

It is the practice of both Roman Catholic and Protestant churches to speak vows at baptisms. If children are not old enough to speak for themselves, oaths are taken by parents and godparents, and the vows are later confirmed by the children themselves. As often as not, the participants are oblivious to the ramifications of not adhering to the vows they made.

Here are some of the components that are affirmed by the candidates for baptism. At infant baptisms, the guardians of the child swear these oaths on behalf of the child:

> I renounce the devil and all of his works. I renounce the sinful desires of the flesh and will not follow them nor be led by them. I accept Jesus as my Savior and Lord. I will obey God's will and commandments and with God's help will walk in the same all the days of my life.

How many people who have sworn that oath—either in baptism or as guardian—have totally reneged on what they promised?

If we consider the number of children who are living unrestrained lives, we realize that it is not only the young people who are suffering. The parents and guardians who swore to teach those children the principles of godly living are equally afflicted for not keeping their vows.

The prophet Malachi stated that the hearts of fathers must focus on the children for whom God holds them responsible lest the earth be smitten with a curse (see Malachi 4:6). Many nations seem to be staggering under the weight of that curse.

In fact, I have no doubt that tied up in the whole package of neglecting baptismal vows are the heartaches of teen suicides, the growing number of teen pregnancies, and the economic and health struggles that so many children and adults face in society today.

Marriage Vows

The divorce rate among Christians almost equals that of non-Christians. In addition, some polls indicate that as many as 50 percent of married women and 60 percent of married men have engaged in extramarital affairs.

Traditional marriage vows remain the most common forms used in ceremonies. They contain vows to marital fidelity that include the phrases *until death do us part* and *as long as we both shall live.*

How rampant are the consequences for breaking marriage vows in our modern society?

Divorce does not disentangle couples who have small children. Rather, it often complicates and amplifies whatever grievances the couple might already have. *As long as we both shall live* is indeed a harsh reality, as estranged parents are forced to interact to deal with the hard issues of child support, visitation and child rearing issues.

As long as we both shall live also frequently includes the curse of developmental trauma that divorces spawn in kids. Those same problems associated with divorce inevitably increase financial stresses. Without the intervention of God, the divorced couple and their children languish in a hostile relational environment, causing everyone involved to experience emotional wounds and trauma.

Regarding infidelity, Hebrews 13:4 gives strong warning that those who defile the marriage bed through adultery will be judged. In Malachi 2:13–16, the prophet denounced spouses who deal treacherously with the marriage partner of their youth, saying that even their blessings will be cursed because of their unfaithful behavior.

The problems attached to infidelity manifest far beyond exasperating arguments and ruined relationships. The apostle Paul warned in 1 Corinthians 6:18 that those who engage in immorality are actually committing sin against their own bodies. Could that be a contributing factor to the rampant number of men and women plagued with cancers in their reproductive organs? Sexual dysfunctions affect both sexes to the point where individuals cannot enjoy marital intimacy. Truly, the breaking of marriage vows through divorce and infidelity produces ghastly repercussions.

We must be certain that we mean what we say. Consider this other common area where vow making can be as detrimental as any of these mentioned so far—and it also happens in church. They are the vows we make to God when singing hymns and choruses. It is rather scary to think what so many vow to do, with hands raised to God, and then promptly forget when exiting the service. As the angel told Daniel, "I have come for your words." It is foolish to sing words in worshipful tones that we do not intend to keep.

Making Ill-Advised Vows

Jesus warned us clearly that we are not to swear oaths or make vows of our own invention. Many people habitually utter oaths with spontaneity in their daily conversations. When we make oaths in God's name, we do so to give our own words more credibility. A frustrated mom tells a teen, "I swear to God, if you do that again you'll be grounded for the rest of your life!" Such vows put God's name to momentary exaggerations. Primarily, it is a form of taking God's name in vain.

Jesus said we will be either justified or condemned by the words we speak. The apostle James reiterated this warning in his epistle. Because our lives are like vapors, he said, we really do not know what the future holds. We should speak humbly about what we will and will not do, making sure to consider God's will as we go about our plans: "You ought to say, 'If the Lord wills, we shall live and do this or that'" (James 4:15).

The implications of an oath suggest that we have the ability to control the future. To make an oath and not keep it is one and the same as swearing falsely. Jesus and James both advised that our statements should stand on their own merits. Anything beyond a yes or a no is an evil statement inspired by the evil one. (See Matthew 5:33–37; 12:37; James 4:13–16; 5:12.)

In recent years, many believers have become aware that it is unwise to connect with organizations through oaths, and have severed their connections. Oaths taken in Masonic Lodges and college fraternal orders are just two examples.

As an example of vows that we should not take, let's look at oaths demanded by some spiritual leaders. There are pastors who solicit lifetime vows of loyalty from their members, and some believers naïvely engage in that degree of commitment. Some believers who have made vows of that sort speak about their pastor's value in their lives in a manner that is normally reserved for Christ.

The Lord is jealous for His people's affections. He will not tolerate a human vessel receiving glory and credit for blessings He alone has wrought in people's lives. I know of a number of people who are encountering self-inflicted curses for making unscriptural vows to their pastors.

Some people wake up to this inappropriate loyalty, discovering that they are living without the freedom and abundance promised to those who place their faith and trust in Jesus Christ. Sometimes that recognition prompts them to leave those situations, facing the possibility of being saddled with a curse from the jilted pastor and fellowship. In too many cases, the roots of identification with their pastors run inordinately deep, and they find it almost impossible to leave.

Christians who are able to break these ungodly vows often find it hard to resettle in authentic Christian fellowships. The result is significant withdrawal from any form of church involvement.

Whenever people in such situations are willing to face their former pastors, I recommend they seek release. In all cases, I lead the individuals in repentance and renunciation of the inappropriate vows they made.

There are extreme situations where it is necessary to break the demonic image of the leader that has been imprinted upon a parishioner's psyche. It requires the courage to shatter the inner images of their former leaders with the hammer of the authority of God's Word. Those kinds of inner images are reminiscent of what Ezekiel 8:3 defines as the image that provokes God to jealousy. Christians are to be conformed to the image of Christ, not to the personality or lifestyle of a particular leader.

Divine Help for Crop Failures

The good news is twofold. First, the love of God covers a multitude of sins and people do not suffer consequences for every vow and oath. Second, where consequences have taken root, the effects of the words can be broken and dramatic reversals can take place in the lives of those who are being affected by them. God is more than willing to intervene in all of the situations we have described where the seeds of a potential curse have been planted. The Lord will graciously facilitate merciful "crop failures" on whatever negative harvests are sprouting in your life. The means He employs to enact those crop failures will be your confession about what the Bible says the blood of Jesus accomplished for you at Calvary.

Here are some preliminary steps to precede the appropriation and application of the blood of Jesus Christ in such situations.

First, identify the fields of your life in which you are experiencing the effects of denouncements and vows. While you are taking stock of those fields, make note of any aspects that smack of the presence of demonic personalities.

Second, if a person cursed you verbally, *and if it is feasible and safe for you to do so*, seek a personal audience with that person. Luke's testimony given above outlines the pattern of asking for that person to recant and withdraw his or her denouncements, as well as engaging in mutual forgiveness and a request for prayers of blessing instead.

Third, if you are divorced, and, again, *if it is feasible and safe for you to do so*, you may want to consider meeting with your former spouse to discuss the consequences from abrogation of your marriage vows. Both parties should repent with godly sorrow for breaking the marriage covenant. Forgiveness should be sought and mutually expressed. Wisdom demands additionally that you both come to equitable agreements about supporting and respecting one another in the handling of child rearing responsibilities.

Fourth, unfulfilled baptismal vows and the broken vows of baptism sponsors must be confessed directly as sins toward God. Forgiveness from the Lord can be obtained instantaneously. Afterward, the baptismal vows should be reaffirmed.

Fifth, consider prayerfully whether or not you have made ill-advised vows. Also consider whether or not you are one who habitually makes spontaneous vows. With unwise vows, repent and renounce the vow you made to any organization or person. Repent of any vow phrases regularly employed in your conversations. Confess faith that the Lord has nullified the effects of whatever your words called for. For example, with "Cross my heart and hope to die," confess a healthy heart and a long life.

Sample Prayer

If you have identified fields where you know the seeds of a curse are at work and you have taken any appropriate steps relationally, the next step is to earnestly repent, confess any related sins, and invoke the forgiveness and power of the blood of Jesus Christ, asking the Lord to bring about "crop failures" among the curses in the fields you have identified.

Here is a sample prayer to help you place that desire before the Lord. It will help you express your thoughts to the Lord in a way that will bring His grace and help.

Heavenly Father, I come to You in Jesus' name. I have discovered that I am suffering the consequences of denouncements and vows. There are fields within my life circumstances that bear the evidences of this. (Name the areas of economic and relational stresses, any adverse health conditions, etc.)

Lord, I need for You to intervene on my behalf. I ask for Your help on the basis of all that Your Son accomplished for me through His atoning blood. At Calvary, He kept His vow of obedience to Your will. Jesus took all of the punishment due me that I might be liberated to enjoy all of the blessings due Him. His cleansing blood is Your divine agent to rectify my situation. I declare that His blood spoils the cursed harvest that I am experiencing. His blood brings true "crop failure" to the consequences of seeds of curses that have been planted in my life.

I declare that I am a new creation in Christ. The denouncements that (name the person) uttered against me cannot thrive where Christ's blood has been applied. Due to Your forgiveness, the vows that I have broken no longer bear witness against me. The ill-advised vows that I have made carry no weight in the courts of heaven. I thank You that I am forgiven for interweaving flippant vows into my conversations. By Your grace I will not suffer any consequences. By the authority of Jesus' name, I command any demonic parasites to leave my soul and body now so that I may be restored to wholeness.

Lord, I humbly accept the truth that Your will for me is spiritual vibrancy, mental acuity, physical health, relational wholeness and financial prosperity. From this time forward, I know that I will be blessed in all of my endeavors and relationships. I thank You, dear Father, for granting me liberation from further harvests of any seeds of curses that have been planted in me. In Jesus' name, Amen!

A Proper Pause Before You Go On

What you have just declared is a powerfully effective prayer that will affect every aspect of your future. Please take a moment to savor the fresh air of freedom and release your prayer has brought to you.

Then take some extra time before going on to the next chapter to thank the Lord again for His power and grace to release you completely from the effects of denouncements and inappropriate vows in your life.

We are now ready to cover a topic about which most of us are all too familiar: control freaks. You will learn how to break the soul ties that keep you in bondage to those manipulating you.

15

Manipulation and Soul Ties

Almost everyone knows someone who needs to be in control, who feels he or she must have the last word. It might be a boss, a "friend," a spouse, even a spiritual leader. People like this are experts at manipulation, and they use a vast and effective arsenal of weapons to persuade and coerce others into compliance. The force at work in them, as we will see in this chapter, is often demonic in origin, and must be dealt with as such.

Manipulative Strategies

Manipulators use various strategies to accomplish their goals. Some play the part of the victim. They comment, with tears, that no one really cares about them. They bemoan how misunderstood and unlovable they are. Family and friends feel obligated to assure them they are loved and valued, and prove it by giving in to their wishes. Some manipulators employ outbursts of anger, scowling expressions and aggressive body language. They often gain control of their families with just a look. Manipulators who have significant verbal skills will sometimes use logic and persuasive arguments to win the day.

Religious manipulators are particularly bold. They twist Scripture and biblical principles to pressure families and spiritual devotees to accept their ideas. They use the name and will of God as their trump cards for almost every situation. Few conscientious believers are bold enough to voice objections when a manipulator declares, "The Lord has spoken." No one wants to argue with God.

Parental manipulators often inflict emotional wounds on their children. Children whose emotions are continually contorted in attempts to convince parents of their affection or win their acceptance are at risk of developing severe insecurity and uncertainty about their identity. In adulthood, those victims have trouble making decisions and commitments.

Manipulation is different from convincing people to embrace an idea through reasoned arguments. The persons who are won over in such cases will not feel pressured and will often feel good about the decisions they have been convinced to make. It is quite another matter when the force of human personality is used to coerce persons against their wills. In those cases, the people who have been "played" never have a sense of satisfaction. Instead, they feel used and abused.

Spiritual Forces Employed

The word *manipulation* is not a biblical term. There is, however, another descriptor for this sinful work of the flesh that is surprisingly akin to it. The term is *witchcraft*.

Witchcraft could be described as the effort to get others to behave in a certain manner through the use of covert mental or spiritual powers. This activity is sinful in that its primary goal is to establish control over another person's actions and thoughts without considering the will of either God or the other party. Anyone who regularly engages in deliberate manipulation can attract spirits of witchcraft.

First Samuel 15:23 notes two common forces behind manipulation.

These two forces, which are described as being the same as witchcraft and idolatry, are rebellion and stubbornness. A rebellious person seeks to establish his will in a situation where the authority belongs to another. A stubborn individual values his personal opinions to the point of overruling any other.

Persons who are operating in witchcraft manipulation are both rebellious and stubborn, subordinating God's will and the wishes of others to their own goals. They consider those in their spheres of influence subservient to them. Their chief pursuit is always to achieve their own self-centered ends.

Spiritual "Umbilical Cords"

Infants in the womb draw life-giving nutrients from their mothers through umbilical cords. At birth, the umbilical cord is severed, separating the infant from that direct lifeline to the mother and symbolically launching the little one into life on his own.

There are also umbilical cords in the realm of the Spirit. Solomon spoke of a silver cord that is detached at death (see Ecclesiastes 12:6). Throughout a person's life that connection extends from the individual's spirit into the presence of God, symbolizing a cord of communication from the Lord with the person's spirit to enrich and sustain his life. At death the silver umbilical cord is severed, and the spirit of a person ascends back to God.

The devil, unlike God, has no respect for a person's free will. For the enemy, the concept of people operating under the influence of God is abominable. Instead, Satan wants to control and dominate people's lives. A major way he does so is by mimicking God's silver umbilical cord phenomenon. He uses something called *soul ties*.

What Is a Soul Tie?

A soul tie is a corrupt spiritual connection between the soul of one individual and the soul of another. When a soul tie has been established, the "infant" end of the connection draws life-influencing powers from the "maternal" end of the connection. Unbeknownst to all involved, the soul of the person on the maternal end has an umbilical attachment to the devil and to his demons of manipulation.

In other words, witchcraft-empowered manipulators are soul-tied to Satan. When the people they have targeted for their manipulation succumb to their influence, soul ties are established. By extension, the individuals are actually creating umbilical soul ties with Satan. In various aspects of life, then, the manipulated persons become dominated not only by the manipulator's witchcraft, but by the devil and his demons. In that event, they are being influenced by Satan rather than by God in whatever venues of life their manipulators control.

The devil is a cruel taskmaster. If he had his way, all of us would have tentacle-like soul ties with multiple individuals who are all soul-tied to himself. His goal is to pervert and to confuse the communications that come from God through the silver cord spoken of in Ecclesiastes.

There are no restrictions on the kinds of human relationships that witchcraft soul ties can affect. Umbilical bondages can be established in a variety of circumstances. It is especially common, for example, for soul ties to be established between former lovers, particularly when the relationship has been long-term and included promises of eternal endearment.

The solution is to employ faith and to sever every suspected soul tie, cutting off the influence of controlling evil spirits of witchcraft.

Activating the Scalpel

There are clear signs of soul ties.

How can you tell if you have been entangled with a soul tie? The main evidence of soul ties with a long-term manipulator is that you feel as though you are living under the manipulator's shadow. In the various tasks of life, you are always haunted by thoughts of whether or not the person with whom you have a soul tie would approve.

It seems like perpetual bondage, and you may feel resentment or general misery. With former lovers, for instance, it can be unwanted sexual fantasies about physical intimacy years after the relationship has ended.

There are several actions required to sever soul ties. The first is to cast out spirits of witchcraft and control. I have found it helpful to use the name of the manipulator when commanding the spirit of witchcraft to depart, such as "I renounce the spirit of witchcraft that operates through Winifred or Herman." Some people's identities are so entwined with their manipulators that there is an imprint of that person's image on their souls. That is why I recommend using the name of the individual.

Next ask the Holy Spirit to cut that person's image out of you. Afterward, envision taking the sword of God's Word to sever the umbilical cord between the two of you. From there, praise God for the fact that all soul attachments have been severed. Thank Him for the reality that your only remaining attachment is that which runs through your silver cord into His glorious presence.

Cutting out or smashing the manipulator's dominant image in your psyche functions as deliverance, but you can command it to leave as a follow-up measure.

It is possible that the manipulators are not aware of the trouble they have caused. If you choose to approach someone for forgiveness, correction and reconciliation, which is scriptural, remember that it is always important to be diplomatic. Any such conversation should take place without accusation or condemnation.

It is also important to be safe. Unfortunately, some people are so addicted to being in control that they will not listen to reason. It may be the case that you should avoid contact with them in all but life-and-death matters. It is a tough call, but this is often necessary to protect one's family and to ensure one's own peace.

Some controllers have a change of heart after long spans of formal separation and become willing to discuss the matter. Most often that happens when those who have broken contact with them pray for them faithfully and persistently.

Interestingly, though, there are times when the most expeditious route is to withdraw prayer from manipulators. If they are accustomed to having others cover them with prayer, they can sense its absence just as significantly as they can miss the physical presence of those whom they have manipulated. Sometimes naked exposure to the price tag for their thirst for dominance is sobering unto repentance.

In the next chapter, we will talk about powers that dominate the lives of millions. Specifically, we will discuss deliverance from the power of sexual perversions.

16

Breaking the Power of Sex Perversions

I was in my early thirties when my cousin, Jeffrey (not his real name), told me he was gay. He said that most of the people to whom he told his secret would begin to lecture him about changing his orientation, and he would counter by going into detail about torrid affairs with well-known individuals who were living double lives.

Jeffrey was caught off guard when I told him that he had always been and would always remain my favorite cousin. With tears in his eyes, Jeffrey told me how his "holier-than-thou" neighbors had persisted in yelling catcalls every time they saw him or his partner. I apologized on behalf of those neighbors. I told Jeffrey that I could give him a biblical explanation for why I believe homosexuality is wrong, but would not do so without his invitation. He sighed with relief, but, frankly, the invitation never came.

The New Testament does not commission Christians to judge and condemn the people of the world for any sins, sexual or otherwise. The apostle Paul stated emphatically that it was not his place or ours to condemn deviant behavior among the unconverted (see

1 Corinthians 5:9–13). We are, however, charged to gently approach fellow believers when it becomes apparent that they are snared by aberrant behavior.

What Sex Symbolizes

After God created Adam and Eve, He commended His handiwork by saying it was very good. The goodness God spoke of included their capacity to enjoy sexual relations. The bond of physical intimacy between a husband and wife typifies the degree of relationship, though non-sexual, that the redeemed are to have with the Godhead through the Holy Spirit (see Ephesians 5:30–32).

Husbands and wives are one flesh. Those who are joined to the Lord are one spirit with Him. Salvation's mystical union unites believers with the Trinitarian oneness of God the Father, God the Son and God the Holy Spirit. The measure of vulnerability and authority that a man and a woman entrust to one another during the intimate act of marriage represents the vulnerability and authority that Christ shares with His Bride, the Church.

Vulnerability and *authority* are appropriate words. Through the mystery of redemption, Christ purposely committed His reputation and divine authority to His Church. The depth of unwavering trust the Godhead has exhibited toward the Church has never been available to Satan or his demons. The devil and his minions, therefore, are insanely covetous of that quality of trust that sexual intimacy between married couples of the opposite sex represents in the eternal realm of the Spirit. That is why demons concentrate so much effort on inserting pollution into sex acts. The unholy and unnatural defilements that mankind invents at the urging of evil spirits are designed to insult God.

Origins of Perversity

Romans 1:18–32 outlines how sex perversions evolved. Subsequent to the fall of Adam, mankind began a downward spiral. The motivating factor was pride. It caused mankind to suppress the truth that God's invisible attributes and the path to godliness can be clearly understood by observing creation. The facets of life that are designed to reflect God's glory are countless. The devil enticed humans to become preoccupied with self-centeredness. One of his first steps was the perversion of sex.

According to the Bible, the natural sexual functions of men and women were exchanged for that which is unnatural. Both sexes began to crave sex acts that were "against nature." At first, the experimentations were likely with those of the opposite sex. Then the practices expanded to those of the same sex. By definition, activities designed to implant seed emitted from the reproductive organs of one sex into that of the opposite sex for fertilization are natural. Emissions with those of the same sex are unnatural.

Rebellion by committing unnatural sex acts led to other sins such as greed, deceit, strife, unforgiveness, violence and hatred for God. Mankind was permitted to go its own way. All the while the voice of conscience warned that those who sow such acts chance reaping self-inflicted judgments.

To make matters worse, humans became so numb to the sensitivities of conscience that they applauded one another's sins and perverse escapades (see Romans 1:32). This has been demonstrated over the past several generations by our educational system and the entertainment industry. Without question, Satan has employed both to serve as his well-oiled misinformation machine. In the name of diversity, schoolchildren are instructed about alternative lifestyles and sexual release techniques. Girls as young as eleven give in to peer pressure to have oral sex—touted in some areas as "the new good-night kiss." Educators and show business personalities assert that homosexuality is a natural choice for individuals predisposed to its inclinations.

Deviant lifestyles, mislabeled as natural, come primarily from the refusal to acknowledge that original sin spawned unnatural desires. The entire creation was subjected to corruption, of which sexual perversity was a part (see Romans 8:20–21). Homosexual behavior in animals, for instance, which is often cited as God's approval of the practice, came subsequent to and is inherent in original sin and the fall of Adam. When God created living things, neither man nor beast had such inclinations.

Unnatural sex acts have all the earmarks of demonic inspiration. Most would agree that immorality is a major means of spreading sexually transmitted diseases. Emergency room workers are well acquainted with some of the more injurious aspects of unnatural sex acts. It is commonplace for them to treat injuries in victims of sadomasochistic sexual encounters and to extract lodged objects from body cavities.

The Problem of Sex Addictions

Sex is an exceptionally strong aspect of the human psyche. Any physical activity that has accompanying pleasurable sensations can become a preoccupation, allowing addiction to spring forth easily. Note that not everyone who engages in sexual perversion is necessarily a sex addict.

Here is the context in which I am using the word *addiction*. It is enslavement to sex to the point that it is no longer regarded as an expression of a holy love-based relationship. Sex addicts' waking hours are spent concentrating on opportunities for self-centered orgasmic release, not unlike heroin addicts escaping life's realities through drugs. More and more pastors are hearing women in their congregations complain about their husbands who are hooked on pornographic websites. The addiction of some is pedophilic. The most common enslavement is the compulsion for individuals of both sexes to act like nomads in a sea of endless sexual partners.

Only satanic influences could possibly lead anyone to believe that some of the practices of unnatural sex acts follow the original design and intention of the Creator. I dealt with one seminary student who was addicted to sex with dead fur-bearing animals.

In the Marriage Relationship

With married couples, the voice of God within is a trustworthy gauge to help discern what is appropriate and what is not. Certainly within the bonds of married love, there is room for variety in the sexual experience. If, however, such experimentation makes either partner uncomfortable, the uneasiness is likely justified. It is sinful to engage in a sexual activity that both partners feel is improper, or with which both are not comfortable to perform in good conscience.

Anyone who continually ignores godly inhibitions is at risk of opening up to spirits of perversion and perhaps sexual addiction. Further enticements for more intense types of experimentation are sure to follow. Astonishingly, for example, there are sophisticated people who are addicted to pain during sex.

Satan's objective is to inundate the marriage bed with activities that cause couples to cast aside all thoughts of holy union. In such instances, many would testify that any momentary gratification they might experience carries a heavy price tag of emptiness of soul the morning after.

The Bible's Challenge

Basically, the claim of Satan's propaganda machine is that sexual abnormalities do not succumb to reparative therapy. That is not what the Bible teaches. In the passage 1 Corinthians 6:9–13, we see a list of unrighteous individuals who will be denied entrance into the Kingdom of God. Fornicators, adulterers, homosexuals, thieves, drunkards and revilers are mentioned specifically. The passage proclaims boldly, however, that these ones can be changed by salvation.

I have added italics to verse 11 to emphasize that after being born again, those who previously sinned in that way *were no longer* ensnared in those sins: "And such *were* some of you. But you *were* washed, but you *were* sanctified, but you *were* justified in the name of the Lord Jesus and by the Spirit of our God."

The implication is that the body is not for immorality, but for the Lord. Believers must not submit to the powers of sin.

Addressing the subject of homosexuality again, we see that in the context of Christianity and the born-again experience, the argument about whether homosexuality is genetic or acquired is rendered moot. Even the rare instances in which a person is born with homosexual desires or tendencies do not provide a free pass to engage in a homosexual lifestyle. It is just as ungodly to live out that tendency toward homosexuality as it is to live out an inborn tendency to be a drunkard. It is not life-threatening to say no to the forbidden behavior for the sake of Christ. One can go to heaven with unfulfilled sexual compulsions. No one can see God unless he or she has reckoned those unlawful passions as dead in the active pursuit of holiness (see Colossians 3:5; Hebrews 12:14).

I suspect that a double standard exists with those who assert they are powerless to control depraved passions. Let us imagine a professing Christian homosexual couple that has one partner who is a thief and is given to abusive speech. It is highly probable that the law-abiding, verbally abused partner would press the offending partner to stop stealing and to control his tongue. Furthermore, he would expect him to succeed at doing so. Biblically, thievery and abusive speech appear in the same list as fornication and homosexuality.

Remember the phrase "such *were* some of you" in 1 Corinthians 6:11? Is there any biblical reason for it to apply to thieves and revilers and not to homosexuals? There is no difference. Sin is sin. Christ within empowers believers to put all sinful inclinations into the past tense.

Deliverance

The first step toward liberation from all forms of sex perversion is to genuinely want deliverance. It is unproductive to submit to deliverance just to please parents or to comply with the wishes of a spouse or to assuage momentary guilt pangs. The primary motive must be the Spirit-inspired conviction that the act at issue insults the holiness of God.

One must be absolutely committed to the reality that the old carnal nature was crucified with Christ at Calvary. That entity is dead and was buried in the waters of baptism. With those factors established, the specific demon of perversity must be expelled. If you are seeking help in this area, treat that demon with utter hatred over the despicable acts it has compelled you to perform. Homosexuals who have participated in "gay pride" events should repent of glorying in that which is shameful (see 1 Corinthians 5:1–2, 6; Ephesians 5:11–12).

When I minister to those given to sex perversions and to sex addicts, I ask them to lay their hands on their erogenous zones, one by one. As they do so, I command the particular evil spirit to leave each location in Jesus' name. In addition, sex addicts I have counseled have described what we might label an erotic energy resident in them. It causes their flesh to tingle with desire for erotic contact. I have them repeat the laying-on-of-hands procedure and ask them personally to command that energy to leave them. They often report that they can feel the demonic force actually slip away.

This chapter has covered some sensitive core issues. It is fitting to spend some time seeking God as to whether or not areas in your life need adjustment. I suggest that you repeat this contemplative prayer several times and then listen for what the Lord might say to you: "I am not my own. I have been bought with a price: the precious blood of Jesus."

Next, we deal with spirits of infirmity. The success rates involved in delivering people of catastrophic illnesses and those with diagnosed mental conditions have been points of substantial challenge. We are making headway, but all of us are still early in the learning curve. To emulate the Master Physician, we are obligated to keep trying, and that is one of the reasons for our next chapter.

17

Dealing with Spirits of Infirmity

In the matter of healing, the Body of Christ has yet to approach anything even close to the ministry of Jesus. No matter what the source
of the malady He confronted, without fail, Jesus healed all who came
to Him. The wide gap between His success rate and our hit-and-miss
attempts would be discouraging were it not for His promise that we
would perform greater miracles than He. That prophecy was not given
for a few gifted individuals. It speaks of the Body of Christ functioning
in the unity of the faith in the fullness of the stature of Jesus Christ.

Spirits of infirmity can be the source of physical maladies and
mental disorders. In other words, anything may be demonic, but
not everything is. One person can have a crippling spirit of arthritis
cast out and be completely restored. Another person can have the
same symptoms and undergo deliverance without experiencing any
changes because the infirmity is not demonic in origin but, rather,
physical.

This means we need to exercise discernment so as to be able to
help guide any person who is suffering into the ministry—spiritual

or medical—that he or she needs. We should never assume every problem comes from demons.

Success Can Be Elusive with Mental Conditions

Over the years, I have attempted deliverance on scores of people with diagnosed mental conditions. On one particular occasion, I ministered to a young autistic boy who was compelled to urinate on bathroom walls. I cast out the demon troubling him, and then his mother and I walked with him to the bathroom where he urinated directly into the toilet. His mother wept for joy. Even though deliverance prayer was successful in this case, I have ministered to several other autistic children without seeing the same dramatic results.

I find this to be the case far too often with conditions that have a mental component. Sometimes people are healed; sometimes they are not. Sometimes the healings "last"; sometimes they do not.

Why is this the case? There are various possible explanations for the failures. The most obvious is that most mental disorders might not be demonic in origin. Perhaps they could be attributed to soul problems that we do not yet know how to unravel. For certain, many dysfunctions of the mind are caused by hormonal and chemical imbalances. In those cases, physical healing is needed.

At the same time, some mental conditions are unquestionably demonic. Why do these not always respond to deliverance? I have observed two consistent obstacles with mental patients for whom all attempts at deliverance have failed.

The first is that the patient himself has not been the one to ask for deliverance. When loved ones bring a person to me, any absence of desire on the part of the patient may be one of the limiting factors.

The second is the majority of the mentally impaired for whom I have prayed are people who refuse to take their prescribed medications. That stubborn resistance to medication, which eliminates or suppresses their symptoms, could be an indication that the patient somehow needs the escape that the symptoms supply. It may be that the drug of choice is the mental disorder itself. This tendency to partner with the illness reveals that in some cases, spirits of infirmity are allowed to stay because the person does not truly desire liberation.

As I have continued to process the challenges I have experienced in this area, I have put two policies into place that I hope will lay the groundwork for more to be set free. These policies are direct results of the obstacles given above.

First, I will not accept appointments with adults who do not request the ministry on their own. Then, they must take their medications for a week prior to and on the day of the appointment. This affords me the opportunity to speak to the person without interference from the mental condition. I will ask them to state specifically what they want to be delivered from and why. I formulate the name of the suspected spirit from what they state. From there, I minister deliverance in my customary fashion. Even after deliverance I do not recommend that mental patients go off their medication without the consent of their physicians.

The Strange Case of Darrell

I was asked a number of years ago to minister deliverance to a man in his twenties named Darrell, who had been diagnosed with obsessive-compulsive disorder. When I arrived at the family's home to pray for Darrell, I found a mind-boggling sight. The home was strewn with open cans of food and partially eaten sandwiches and fruit.

As it turned out, Darrell would not eat anything without first washing each bite while standing at the kitchen sink. If the food came from a can, after several small portions were consumed, he considered what remained of the food in the can to be unclean. A fresh can of the same food would have to be opened for him to continue eating. The same rules applied to bites from apples and from a single bunch of grapes. Three bites maximum from a whole fruit; three grapes maximum from a single bunch; then the uneaten portions were discarded.

Darrell was grossly underweight. He compulsively splashed water on himself dozens of times throughout the day and night. The tangled hair that hung down his back was always damp. The radio and TV were incessantly blaring Christian programming. Darrell's fears of contamination had kept him homebound for years. Instantly, I discerned that Darrell's OCD condition was perpetrated by a spirit of infirmity called religious confusion.

My first step was to ask his mother to turn off the blaring TV and radio. Then I turned my attention to Darrell.

"Darrell," I asked, "are you willing to do everything I direct you to do in order to be set free?"

"Yes," he replied.

"Your OCD is actually a religious demon," I said. "I am going to command it to leave you." I explained further that after his deliverance I was going to offer food to him to eat, and then we were going to make a trip to the barber.

Darrell gazed back at me with a puzzled but agreeable expression.

"After your deliverance," I continued, "you are welcome to go to church once per week. However, I want you to agree that you will not watch or listen to Christian programming for six months. Are you willing to comply with my prescriptions?"

"Yes, I am willing," Darrell agreed.

Then I continued my ministry to Darrell by praying directly against the spirit that was troubling him.

"You spirit of confused OCD infirmity," I commanded, "you foul spirit of religious confusion, come out of Darrell now!"

With a series of coughs and huffs of breath that he forcefully exhaled, Darrell expelled that demon.

The first proof of his deliverance came when Darrell ate mouthful after mouthful of peanuts that I handed to him, something he never would have done in his previous OCD condition. His mother giggled with glee.

A few minutes later we pulled into a fast-food restaurant, and Darrell ravenously consumed a burger and fries and licked the ketchup that was dripping from his fingers.

The haircut was the icing on the cake, absolutely transforming Darrell's appearance.

For Darrell, there would be no more ritualistic food cleansings. What's more, his compulsion to splash water over himself evaporated. The family home became as neat as a pin. Jesus had set Darrell completely free from OCD.

Physical Infirmities

In contrast to deliverance ministry to those with mental problems, deliverance seems more likely to succeed when dealing with spirits of physical infirmities. Many people seem to have much greater success in this area.

A woman came with her sister one day to get food at our church's food bank. The sister was totally blind. When they asked for prayer, I asked how long the woman had been blind and was told two months. I inquired about diabetes and other health issues, but nothing seemed related. Then I asked about what happened at the time of the onset of the blindness, and the woman said that it had occurred instantly. "I got real mad at my kids, and it happened as I was screaming at them."

Clearly, the expression, "I'm so mad, I can't see," was more than a colloquialism in this case. I commanded the demon of "hysteric conversion" that had frozen her optic nerves to come out. The woman was healed instantly.

For some reason, one area of particular ability for me is praying for people with headaches, fevers, unexplainable chronic pains and allergies. In the allergies department, especially effective have been my prayers against allergies caused by natural substances. I have seen many delivered of spirits that cause reactions to pollen, pet hair, dust and the like. Other people seem also to have areas in which they "specialize."

I believe that Jesus invented the specialist concept in order for the Body's members to be interdependent, one upon another. First Corinthians 12:28 speaks of "gifts of healings," not one gift of healing. More people would probably be healed if we disciplined ourselves to discern each individual, unique healing anointing.

When dealing with spirits of infirmity, I verbally rebuke those spirits with biblical phrases about spiritual authority and healing. My strategy includes speaking not only to the evil spirit, but also to the location in the body where it is causing discomfort. The following is an example of how I might pray in the case of someone with a spirit of allergies to grain foods. Let's call the person we are ministering to by the name of Jane.

"God has given us all foods to enjoy. Bread strengthens the heart and is made from grains. Jane's body is the temple of the Holy Spirit. It has been redeemed and cleansed by the blood of the Lamb.

"I call for the peace of God that surpasses human understanding to flow throughout Jane's digestive organs. God's peace coupled with the power of the blood of Jesus renders powerless this spirit of allergies to grain.

"I speak to Jane's stomach and intestines now. You are reverberating with God's power. You will now eject the spirit of infirmity. You demon of allergies, I command you to leave Jane in Jesus' name.

"Itching and hives will cease and desist. The grace of God has empowered Jane to eat what she pleases when she pleases. Whatever she chooses to eat is sanctified by Christ from this time forth."

Allergic reactions vary from minor to life threatening. In Jesus' day, people showed themselves to the priests to verify healing. Authentic faith is not dampened when a believer with severe reactions has his healing certified by a physician. I do not encourage people with histories of anaphylactic episodes to experiment with foods without the consent of their doctors.

Dealing with Spirits of Pain

I pray for spirits of chronic pain in much the same way as the prayer example above. As a result, I have seen many of those spirits put to flight. In the course of praying, I inevitably call for the location of the body where the pain exists to align itself with the prayers of deliverance.

With headaches, for instance, I speak to the brain before casting out the spirit of migraines. I call for any swelling and excess of fluids to abate. By God's grace, there is seldom a headache that does not instantly succumb to the authority of that prayer.

Cancer situations, on the other hand, are a different story. Cancer is somewhat of an enigma. I confess that most cancer patients who come to me for healing are not healed, yet I have seen a handful of people whom I have prayed for experience remarkable recoveries from the late stages of cancer.

My layman's definition of *cancer* is "cells in rebellion." I believe that in most instances, rebellious spirits of infirmity inhabit those cells. Some authorities say cancer is a virus, and that interferon is a natural antiviral protein produced by cells in the body to inhibit the replication of the virus in other cells. When praying for cancer victims, I speak to the cells of their bodies and instruct them to release interferon, commanding the antiviral protein to speed to every cell. While envisioning that happening by faith, I command the rebellious spirit of infirmity to come out of the patient. In doing so, I call it by the name of whatever form of cancer has been diagnosed.

An example of such a prayer would be the following: "You rebellious spirit of melanoma, I command you to cease your rebellions and to exit in Jesus' name. I stand against you. The Spirit of Jesus Christ is against you. The interferon in this person is empowered by the Holy Spirit. That interferon wards you off and you are suspended with no place to go but out. You are expelled now in Jesus' name."

Those who are serious about seeing the release of a greater number of healings must learn to think outside of the box. God is the Lord

193

of creativity. Out-of-the-box thinking is His home turf. He proved that when He chose you and me.

Continue to Learn

In cases where I have not been successful in praying for physical and mental maladies and their relation to deliverance, I consider that, apparently, I do not have sufficient knowledge or anointing yet to bring about such cures. Even then, however, I do not permit my disappointments to hinder me from pressing onward to learn all I can about Jesus' desire to heal.

I urge you to experiment with the innovative spiritual dynamics for healing that come to your mind and spirit as you seek the Lord. It is highly possible those creative thoughts you receive will be authored by God. Faith demands the willingness to take risks. Take the risks and watch as the Lord causes the world to marvel through His greater release of miraculous cures.

As I said earlier, I am looking forward to improvement in my success rate in many realms of infirmity. One area, however, where my success rate has been 100 percent—and yours can be, too!—is the topic of the next chapter. "Expelling Home-Wrecking Demons" deals with praying through homes and cleansing properties from evil spirits.

18

Expelling Home-Wrecking Demons

Satan's initial attack on mankind was against a relationship. He set the first couple at odds with each other, culminating in Adam's blaming Eve for his own sin. "It was that woman You gave me" was Adam's excuse to God. With that statement, Satan's major objective had been achieved. He had inserted disunity into the relationship of Adam and Eve and into their relationship with God.

The nature of the Serpent has not changed. He is waging the same war today by destroying the concept of the Christian home as God intended it to be. Demons are often the secret agents Satan uses to provoke disharmony and wreck God-ordained home life.

The devil is particularly threatened by the harmonious relationships of people living under the same roof because their close exposure heightens the probability that his works will be exposed. Individuals in close proximity are more likely to communicate their observations and come into prayer agreement about strategies to disrupt the enemy's plans. Satan will, therefore, insert whatever he can to create mayhem in the lives of any home he can—whether singles sharing an apartment, working moms with kids at home, newly married couples or empty nesters.

Skewed Perspectives

It should pain us to confess that Christian homes are often just as disharmonious as those of our unconverted neighbors. We begin our downhill slide by accepting "formulas" that we think will help create heaven on earth. It is not long, however, before the constant assault of demonic pressure turns these ideals toward legalism, and the outcome is just the opposite.

I want to focus on one skewed perspective, because it is so prominent. It is this: "In my home it's God first, family second and vocations third." This, like some other formulas, is not a bad formula. But when any good creed is enacted in a legalistic way, the results misrepresent everything God has designed a home to be. It can create a sense of dissatisfaction with life if one feels guilt for neglecting spiritual matters.

The problem here is that much of Christian teaching separates secular activities from spiritual pursuits. Spiritual things come first; secular things follow. This is a skewed perspective. God did not design life to be compartmentalized. All of life is spiritual.

God planted the first couple in a garden, not in a church sanctuary. He was looking for productivity. Thus His design allows for latitude in the way we approach our worship, our relationships and our work. It is appropriate for any one of these godly priorities to take the lead at given times. Proverbs 24:27, for example, implies that wisdom dictates seasons when work becomes the priority in order later to provide time for the home.

> Prepare your outside work,
> Make it fit for yourself in the field;
> And afterward build your house.

Likewise, family activities will at times supersede spiritual activities (see 1 Corinthians 7:33). The Lord is not offended by where we place the emphasis as long as we acknowledge Him in all of our ways.

Again, the reason I am focusing on this is because I have found that contention over how an ideal Christian home should look is one of the most consistent problems for believers. From the wife's perspective, the husband is not spiritual enough. From the husband's perspective, excessive spiritual chatter is boring. From the children's perspective, Christian parents are too spiritual, often citing "God's will" and "pleasing the Lord" as the reasons for restrictions of their privileges and freedoms. (Consequently, many kids grow up to believe God is a fun-spoiler.) More and more unmarried Christian couples choose simply to live together in order to dodge the mess they have seen that marriage can become.

The devil gets right into the middle of all this, stirring up unreasonable demands for achieving a "Christian home." Then the enemy assigns demonic troublemakers to keep tempers and emotions at the boiling point. Demons of religiosity relish opportunities to use a parent to drive the family to distraction by incessant insistence on spiritual activities. (At the end of this chapter, I will offer some suggestions on how to counter their devices.)

Ways Demons Create Disharmony

Satan's secret home-wrecking agents have free rein in the atmospheres of many homes, particularly when it comes to planting seeds of discord or spotlighting personality conflicts. Demons, for instance, often manipulate parents to whisper discontently about their spouses to their children, with the twisted logic of trying to get the kids on their side. But by doing so, parents are enabling evil spirits to gang up on the other partner and implant emotional wounds and confusion in the children. Little girls are especially vulnerable to arguments between moms and dads. In counseling sessions, women often speak about fears that history is repeating itself in their own troubled marriages. I have seen them cover their ears as they recall their parents screaming at each other.

The objective of these demonic infiltrators goes beyond wounding particular individuals. Their far greater goal is to discredit the reputation of God as Father and Creator of the family.

Here is just one example of demons at work in a home. Fathers are commanded in Scripture not to discourage their children or to provoke them to anger. One way they frequently violate this command is by expecting their children to know what they are thinking without bothering to tell them.

Suppose, for example, a father has not instructed his son in the identification of tools or how to perform specific tasks. Yet the impatient father expects young Johnny to know the difference between pliers and wrenches.

"Johnny, give me the three-eighths ratchet wrench. No, not the pliers, the ratchet wrench. I said the ratchet wrench."

Johnny makes a second try.

"Here it is, Daddy. I got it for you."

"Does that look like a three-eighths fitting? That is the three-sixteenths ratchet fitting. Are you so stupid? Can't you ever do anything right? Never mind. I'll get it myself."

The scene repeats through life, and Johnny continues to be crushed by his dad's comments. At some point, he begins to believe himself to be what his dad has said or implied: He is a stupid idiot who cannot do anything right. Because every child thrives on parental approval and wilts under harsh disapproval, the thoughts batter the child's little soul.

Demons of self-hatred and insecurity hover around him. Johnny will have a hard time believing that God is caring and compassionate, even though the family gets all dressed up for church every Sunday, careful to start the week by "putting God first."

Most people do not understand that it is evil spirits that frequently spark the clashes in relationships. As we said earlier, the work of demons goes far beyond stirring up trouble in our homes. Satan wants to prove that the Lord is incapable of producing any semblance of ongoing joy in the home.

Solutions

There are two biblical components that Christians would do well to incorporate into their philosophies of family life and relationships. One is from the apostle Paul and the other from King Solomon. I believe that commitment to these precepts is a prerequisite to defeating demonic home-wreckers. Prudence and I adopted the principles early in our marriage, and they have served us well for nearly fifty years.

Paul's basic assessment of the home is conveyed in 1 Corinthians 7:28, his summary of the question of whether to marry or not. It is this: Single or married, we will have trouble in life's relationships. Paul was simply serving notice that even godly relationships go through trials. Interestingly, he makes no implication that the presence of trouble indicates the absence of God. He says trouble in relationships is normal.

In Solomon's assessment, some of it rather negative, life can be filled with futility and hardships. God's wisdom gave him the antidote, and it is this component that I suggest you incorporate into your philosophy of a godly home. Summarizing the truths found in Ecclesiastes 5:18–20 and 9:7–10, we find that, first, our godly heritage is to rejoice in the fruits of our labors. We can approach our lives free from legalism to spiritual activities, free to enjoy the good things God has given us. And along with that, if we enter the covenant of marriage, we should enjoy the spouse God has given all of the days of our lives.

The combination of Paul's and Solomon's perspectives will keep you from dwelling on life's hardships and give you a reasonable approach to your home life. This will also serve to immunize you, so to speak, from the deceptions of demons that are out to destroy that which God has called good in your life.

Hardships in life are inevitable. Take them by faith as they come. Do not resent the need to focus temporarily on one priority—such as work—above others, realizing that all of your life is spiritual. Joyfully anticipate the fruits of your labors. It is your heritage to enjoy a godly home. And, praise God, a godly home does not equate to a hyper-religious home.

Expelling Home Wreckers

The atmospheres of troubled homes are filled with home-wrecking spirits that incite the problems. If this is your situation, the demons can be banished. Simply pray through your house, rebuking and expelling the spirits causing upheaval, and then offer praise for God's victory in cleaning out your home.

The rooms in which the conflicts normally occur should be targeted. Pray through the rooms, expelling the spirits by name or by the nature of the disruptions they are causing. For example: "You spirits inciting accusation, anger, alienation, disrespect, bickering, backbiting, hostility, hatred, rejection, religiosity, divorce, etc." If you are praying through the house with young children present, simply describe the demons as bad things that are stirring up trouble.

I realize that my remedy sounds simplistic, but it has stood the test of time. Throughout the years, Prudence and I have periodically found it necessary to cleanse our home once again. The results never cease to amaze us.

Recently, I was asked by a sophisticated couple on the brink of divorce to pray through their home and expel home-wrecking pests. Adultery, pornography and matriarchal manipulation were among the issues they were dealing with.

I went from room to room, into every closet and out into the yard. No demon was exempt from my prayers as I invoked the power of God's authority. Previous to that time of prayer, the husband had viewed the Bible as confusing. Following that prayer, he has made comments about how most every portion he reads is God's special message to him. The marriage is making giant leaps toward recovery.

19

Deliverance from
the Powers of Iniquity

When Wilbur called for a counseling session, I had been studying the topic of iniquity. Pride is a major component of iniquity, and it is iniquity that begets sins in the heart of mankind. I would not classify iniquity as a demon, but I believe that we can be delivered from it nonetheless. Iniquity seems to be a spiritual power that is an aspect of the carnal nature residing in mankind before regeneration of salvation by faith in Christ Jesus. With most people it is ejected along with the "old man" at salvation. With others, however, residues of it are left behind and become problematic throughout their Christian lives.

My meditations on iniquity prior to Wilbur's call had led me to a number of conclusions.

1. Lucifer was an anointed cherub who lost his place in God's Kingdom when iniquity arose from within him (see Ezekiel 28:13–19; Isaiah 14:12–15).

2. The iniquity in Satan drove him to make five prideful "I will" declarations against God.

3. Iniquity is the nature of Satan that governs rebellion and pride in the souls of mankind.

4. Our iniquities separate us from God, and iniquity's pride begets sorrows in our lives.

5. Deliverance from iniquity is possible and advantageous for those who want to please God.

Wilbur's Deliverance from Iniquity

Everything Wilbur spoke the day he came for his appointment blared out the presence of iniquity and perverted pride. Wilbur was a Baptist pastor whose hobby was bodybuilding. He confessed that though he was not a practicing homosexual, he inordinately enjoyed having men gawk at his body while he flexed at the gym.

He then bemoaned how his two teenaged daughters seemed to be sex-crazed. In defiance of Wilbur's and his wife's pleadings, their girls chose provocative attire designed to stir lewd glances and remarks from boys. His sorrow was that they had become sexually active at incredibly young ages. Wilbur mentioned that they had made sexual advances toward older married men.

As Wilbur told his story, a phrase came to me from Job 41:34: "He is king over all of the children of pride." I instantly recognized that the Holy Spirit was telling me that Wilbur's problems were somehow entwined with iniquity's pride. Based upon that revelation, I did not feel directed by the Lord to pray for deliverance from demons in Wilbur's case. To me, evidence was mounting that seemed to indicate that his problem went deeper than anything that classic deliverance from an evil spirit could handle. During our time together, I explained to Wilbur what I had learned about iniquity and told him that my suspicions were that he was struggling with the nature of the calloused pride of Satan within him. He agreed with my conclusions. What transpired when I ministered to him was truly wonderful to experience.

The first step in my prayer for Wilbur was to speak directly to the problem troubling him.

"You iniquity-driven power of pride, I command you to loose my brother's soul right now in Jesus' name. The fingers of God's Spirit hook around you with the authority of Jesus' resurrection, and I draw you out of Wilbur's personality now in the name of the Lord Jesus."

When I made that declaration, Wilbur collapsed onto the floor. I stood at his head and continued to command the powers of iniquity to leave him. To my shock, in the Spirit it felt like I had a huge sailfish on a deep-sea fishing line. As unusual as it may sound, I actually felt a struggling resistance to my commands that was stronger than most anything I had encountered in deliverance up to that point. Suddenly, Wilbur cried out in agony, grabbing his crotch and then his chest. He said it felt as though the powers of iniquity were clawing to keep their place within him.

"I pull all of the powers of iniquity out now."

Suddenly, it felt as though my Spirit-assisted commands had succeeded in loosening iniquity's grip. Wilbur's jaws stretched widely open and several successive streams of a watery substance squirted from the back area of his mouth. I estimate that the thin streams shot about six feet into the air. After that, Wilbur began praising God as he lay on the floor before me.

I do not believe nor have I experienced that Wilbur's deliverance is the template for others to be set free from the powers of iniquity. I am persuaded that what happened with Wilbur had a higher purpose. It was designed to impress me with the reality of some people's need of deliverance from iniquity.

I saw Wilbur frequently after that session. He testified that he was entirely free from the desire to draw the attentions of men. Thankfully, he reported that the behavior of his daughters had also tamed down considerably.

Iniquity and Sin

The Bible mentions *iniquity* 317 times. It also speaks of how the mystery of iniquity will dwell within the individual that the Bible calls the Antichrist. There are certainly mysterious aspects of iniquities that are not understood by most Christians. There are, however, many essential facts that we can and should know about the perils of the power of iniquity.

Iniquity is not one and the same as *sin*. Iniquity births sin. The best treatment of *iniquity* that I have found is in *Dake's Annotated Reference Bible*. In the next section, I provide a summation of what I gathered from Dake's notes and my studies of Bible verses about iniquity-hardened hearts.

The Hebrew word for *iniquity* is *avon*. One of its definitions is "perverseness; to be bent or crooked." Some modern versions of the New Testament translate the Greek word for *iniquity* as "lawlessness." Iniquity is the nature of the lawless devil working in the dispositions of the disobedient to drive them to commit sins.

The Greek word for *sin* is *hamartia*. It has a root that is commonly understood as "missing the mark." Jesus came to bless us by empowering us to turn from our iniquity. The turning is apparently a progressive work. We see this in the book of Hebrews, which encourages us to lay aside every weight and the sin that so easily ensnares us (see Hebrews 12:1). The implication is that it is possible to have strong residues of iniquity within us after salvation.

The goal of the redeemed person should be righteous behavior. Some people continually miss the mark of righteousness in given areas because they have crooked deposits of iniquity in them. It might be said that some are shooting their best intentions through iniquity-bent barrels that cause the continual result of *hamartia*—missing the righteous targets at which they are aiming. The solution is for them to ask God for deliverance from their iniquity so that they will no longer miss the mark of godly living.

Iniquity-Hardened Hearts

It is possible to frustrate the grace of God in our lives. It happens when Christians have a form of godliness, but deny the power of grace to change them (see Galatians 2:21; 2 Timothy 3:5). Somehow these Christians take repentance too lightly, figuring they will always be welcomed at the throne of grace. They do not realize that the ability to repent is a gift that God grants. There are no guarantees that the ability one has to repent on one day will be there the next (see 2 Timothy 2:24–26). There are harsh penalties for discounting the grace of God and for permitting lawless iniquity to rule one's life.

> Of how much worse punishment, do you suppose, will he be thought worthy who has trampled the Son of God underfoot, counted the blood of the covenant by which he was sanctified a common thing, and insulted the Spirit of grace?
>
> HEBREWS 10:29

> "Many will say to Me in that day, 'Lord, Lord, have we not prophesied in Your name, cast out demons in Your name, and done many wonders in Your name?' And then I will declare to them, 'I never knew you; depart from Me, you who practice lawlessness!'"
>
> MATTHEW 7:22–23

The King James Version of the Bible renders *lawlessness* at the end of verse 23 as *iniquity*. For those who have allowed iniquity to harden their hearts, it is not safe to assume that performing dynamic signs equates to God's approval. Miracles are demonstrations of God's mercies toward the needy. They speak volumes about God's grace, but should not be interpreted as attestations of God's favor upon the vessels used to minister the wonders.

The prophet Job declared that God inquires after iniquity (see Job 10:6). The Lord is committed to exposing our iniquities so that we can cooperate with Him in dealing with them. Micah 7:19 states that God "will again have compassion on us, and will subdue our iniquities."

The verb *subdue* can be translated "to violate." Any who have residual iniquities active within them need to have them violated by the power of the Holy Spirit. The high priest Joshua is spoken of in Zechariah 3:1–5. The Lord caused Joshua's iniquities to pass from him and gave him a new garment. That procedure is alluded to in Romans 6:19. Those who have formerly yielded their bodies to iniquity are to yield their bodies to become servants of righteousness. That is what it means to put on Christ. It requires that we own up to the frequent instances where we make decisions to comply with the press of iniquity within us.

The Satanic Phrase "I Will"

When iniquity was activated within Lucifer, he made five assertions using the statement *I will*. The assertions exemplified Satan's dissatisfaction with his God-appointed functions. With each of those assertions, he demonstrated the prideful intention to exert his will over God's will (see Isaiah 14:12–15).

This is a reality that all those desiring deliverance from sin-spawning iniquity must face. Most probably, they have spoken an inward *I will* that is driven by iniquity prior to each engagement in sin. The sin could be indulgence in crack cocaine or exploration of a pornographic website. Whatever the sin, in the moment before it takes place, that person has willfully chosen iniquity over righteousness. To do so continually, especially with presumptuous thoughts that God is obligated to overlook sin, is the height of iniquity at work. It is a blatant display of dragon-like satanic pride. Repentance is the beginning place of cooperation with God so that He can "do violence" to the drive of iniquity within us and cause it to pass from us.

Deliverance from Iniquity

High residual deposits of iniquity can be discerned in others most readily if the "candidate" has an unusual demeanor of pride. Those who are afflicted with intensities of the powers of iniquity seem to sense themselves superior to others. As I have preached and ministered on this topic over the past thirty years, I have seen many resonate with the reality of its power at work in their lives.

By experience, I believe that the power can be cast out. Those who do not receive personal ministry can succeed at conquering it by embracing the cross, which over time will take the wind out of the sails of iniquity drives.

In private sessions, I go after iniquity much like I would a demon, though I do not believe it is a demonic power per se. I reserve ministry from iniquity for situations where classic deliverance from demons has not been effective, or where I specifically discern that iniquity drives are lurking.

Before I minister deliverance from iniquity to anyone, I thoroughly explain what I have outlined in this chapter. I tell the person how the drive of iniquity produces sin. I also correlate iniquity to the prideful "I wills" of Lucifer and the possible presence of powerful residues of iniquity within the individual. I outline to the person I am counseling my clear expectation that God will greatly diminish the power of iniquity to drive them into habitual sins in accordance with our prayers of agreement.

I have never again witnessed another person squirt liquid from his mouth as Wilbur did. But numerous people have experienced extreme dizziness while the Holy Spirit violated the iniquity within them and was causing it to pass from them.

In public mass ministry settings, I preach about iniquity, lead people in a renunciation of it, and then command iniquity to leave them. Most important, whether in private ministry sessions or in public venues, deliverance from iniquity has proved beneficial to many of God's people. The main testimony I have received from those who have reported back has been that freedom from iniquity's prideful rebellions initiated a new epoch of freedom from old sins in their lives.

In our next chapter, we will explore further details about the insidious work of the devil through spirits of antichrist.

20

Battling Spirits of Antichrist

Spiritual warfare is different from earthly warfare. There are no truces and no furloughs. No matter how many victories are won, the war will not be over until the end of this age. At that point, Christ will personally intervene with the power of His wrath, and Satan and his hordes will be chained in hell. The closer we come to that event, the harder the devil will fight, doing so out of the realization that his time is short. In retaliation for the skirmishes won by God's army, Satan will send more and more troops into the fray (see Revelation 12:9–13, 17).

Satan's rage will be fueled by the fact that there will be a massive ingathering of souls for Christ prior to His Second Advent. The devil's response will be to perpetrate a great falling away. Many who have been in the faith will purposely walk away from Christianity. Satan will marshal increasing numbers of a special category of evil spirits to pressure Christians into apostasy. These are spirits of antichrist. (See Matthew 24:3–12, 24; 2 Thessalonians 2:1–4; 1 Timothy 4:1–3; 1 John 2:18–19; 4:1–3.)

The assignment of God's army is to rescue as much of the

end-time harvest of souls as we can from Satan's grip. To do that we must understand the objectives of antichrist spirits, and how and where they operate.

The prefix *anti* implies "something that is against, opposing, opposite, in contrast, a substitution." *Christ* means "anointed." Spirits of antichrist, then, incite people to react against and to invent substitutions for all that pertains to the anointed one, the Messiah, Jesus Christ. This includes His righteous teachings, His anointed delegates, born-again Christians and His natural kinsmen, the Jews.

Daniel 7:25 says that the antichrist spirit will "wear out" the saints. The original language implies that the wearing-down process is mental and emotional. All Christians will periodically feel wearying antichrist oppression. Many new converts will need deliverance from various types of spirits of antichrist—and so will many longtime Christians who have given in to pressures from antichrist spirits.

Antichrist spirits can function like most any type of evil spirit. The key elements distinguishing them from common demons are that they give their hosts inner compulsions to question, discredit, mock and give up on faith in Christ. A spirit of antichrist will attempt to persuade anyone it oppresses that his or her godly efforts have been for naught. Its primary goal is to undermine the reliability of Christ and the Word of God.

The Flood of Antichrist Spirits

Over the past four decades most societies have been hit by an ever-increasing convergence of antichrist spirits coming from seemingly unrelated streams. In the United States, these are the realm of the occult; Islam; the anti-God, "politically correct" postures of the educational system; the liberal news media; influences in the government; and the entertainment industry. The assaults from multiple fronts make countless believers feel overwhelmed. They succumb to thoughts that the Christian life is too tough, that it does not really work, and then they melt into hopelessness without any energy for future battles.

Exposure to antichrist and anti-God philosophies predisposes people to have mindsets that are resistant to biblical truth, allowing evil spirits to be imparted more easily. American schoolchildren are studying a curriculum from educators who have done everything possible to eradicate references to Christ and the God of creation. *In God we trust* was once the benchmark of our government. Today the politically correct are expunging Christian symbols and biblical texts from the halls of government, our national parks and military cemeteries. Many of the entertainment industry's most popular comedians and scriptwriters major on belittling anything that pertains to Christians and to faith in God. It is hard to comprehend how many people have gulped in spirits of antichrist while feeding on a constant diet of mockery of holy matters.

Here is a closer look at two of these streams—Islam and the entertainment industry's sudden fascination with and promotion of vampirism.

The Antichrist Spirit of Islam

Strategic to Satan's ploy to wear down the saints through spirits of antichrist is the promotion of Islam in our world. Islam is the epitome of the manifestation of antichrist spirits. Its founder, Mohammad, claimed to be the superior successor and substitute for the apostleship of Jesus Christ. The Bible says that whoever denies the Father-Son relationship between God and Jesus is of the Antichrist (see 1 John 2:22–23). The Arabic inscription on the Dome of the Rock mosque in Jerusalem says *Allah has no son*. Most anyone familiar with the barbarisms of Shariah law could confirm that Islam is a horrid religion.

Islam has a stifling effect on the prosperity of nations where it becomes a major influence. The antichrist spirits of Islam wear populations down by causing formerly prosperous people to lose incentive for creativity. Within two hundred years of Islam becoming dominant in a previously Christian nation, its intolerance for other religions, its gender bias and its societal restrictions smother cultural advancements.

Islam boasts a "Golden Age of Islam" between the eighth and twelfth centuries wherein it supposedly led the world in science, math and other academic fields. On the contrary, however, nations such as Egypt, Turkey, Syria, Iraq and Iran were Christianized prior to Islamization; the innovations were already in progress before the Muslim takeover.

More importantly, Muslims do not have any reasonable explanations for why the advancements suddenly stopped in those nations after the twelfth century. With the head start Islamic countries were afforded, it should have been they who led the world in industrial, technological and medical advancements. But it was not. It was Christian nations that did so. Were it not for the innovations adopted from Christianized countries, the Muslim nations would still be sitting in the dust of seventh-century Arab culture.

Prosperous nations such as America need to realize that it is risky business to favor Islam and to discount the blessings Christianity has brought. We will consider four examples: Christian Italy against Islamic Turkey, and Christian Spain against Islamic Egypt. All four nations were among the earliest countries evangelized by the apostles.

In Turkey, the Eastern Orthodox Church exercised great influence until the country came under full Muslim rule in the tenth century. Italy became and remains the seat of the Roman Catholic Church.

According to the *2010 World Almanac*, the gross domestic product (GDP) of present-day Islamic Turkey is $903 billion. The literacy rate is 89 percent. The infant mortality rate is 37 deaths per 1,000 births.

In Christian Italy, the GDP is $2 trillion. The literacy rate is 99 percent. The infant mortality rate is 5.6 deaths per 1,000 births.

Now look at Egypt and Spain. Egypt was a Christian nation until it was overthrown by Islam in the eighth century. Its Christian population, the Copts, became a persecuted minority. The GDP of present-day Muslim-ruled Egypt is $444 billion. The literacy rate is 72 percent. The infant mortality rate is 28.4 deaths per 1,000 births.

Spain was a Christian nation until it was conquered by the Jihad hordes in the ninth century. King Ferdinand overthrew Muslim rule, however, in the thirteenth century, and Spain has been predominately Christian ever since. Christian Spain's GDP is $1.4 trillion. The literacy rate is 97 percent. The infant mortality rate is 4.3 deaths per 1,000 births.

Any comparison between Christian nations and Islamic nations, including those that produce oil, shows in every instance that Christianized nations beat the GDPs, literacy rates and infant mortality rates of Islamic strongholds. The statistics prove that nations that have remained Christian and those that have thrown off the shackles of Islam are decisively more blessed and prosperous than Islamic stronghold nations. Islam paves the way for the eventual emergence of the Antichrist by impoverishing populations. In hope of relief from their misery they will accept the Antichrist as their global ruler.

The Antichrist Spirit of Vampirism

Antichrist spirits are making inroads in the entertainment industry through the current explosion of vampire movies and books. The Internet features websites for scores of vampire clubs. For many, the clubs go beyond mere fantasies about sex with flesh-biting, blood-sucking mystical creatures. The members in these clubs actually play roles as vampires and victims. Some of the people involved have actually reported success in conjuring vampire incubi and succubi for wild episodes of sex. We will first discover how vampirism is antichrist in nature and then we will discuss the dangers of its accompanying sexual spirits.

Mockery at Heart
Vampirism is an antichrist mockery and repudiation of the most sacred beliefs of Christianity.

Jesus is the Light of the World. Believers who walk in the light of Christian fellowship are continually cleansed of sins by the blood of Jesus. Acceptance of Jesus guarantees eternity in the glorious light of heaven where there is no darkness of night.

In contrast to the light experienced in Christ by believers, vampires love darkness. Not only that, but light, according to their lore, actually destroys them. Satanic vampire entities seek an environment of activities that can only be conducted in darkness forever. The "eternal life" that vampires promise demands continual sexual relations and bloodletting.

Regarding Holy Communion, the wine and the bread symbolize the blood and flesh of Jesus. Believers partake of the elements to refresh their holy spiritual union with Christ and with Christians who are alive and those who have passed on. In contrast, a male or female vampire interacts with its victim by biting, sucking the blood and sometimes eating the flesh. The feast culminates with physical sex. The victims who allow this to happen believe they will also live forever by becoming vampires themselves and then doing the same to other victims.

A wooden cross symbolizes the sacrificial death of Jesus. Christians are to embrace the cross and to say no to wanton desires. Vampires fear all that is symbolized by crucifixes and wooden stakes. Christians identify with Jesus' death on a wooden cross by saying no to wanton desires. Vampires take human lives to sustain their own as they fulfill their twisted sexual desires. A wooden stake driven through a vampire's heart ends its hope of an eternity of decadence.

Vampirism is a particularly graphic negation of Jesus Christ and all that He represents. The Lord Jesus shed His blood as an act of love to impart eternal life. Vampires take blood through biting and defiled lovemaking to live on eternally.

Fantasies Made Real

Through involvement with the occult and engaging in vampire fantasies, people not only attract demons, but many of these individuals purposely summon demons to themselves. Children as young as thirteen are intrigued rather than repulsed by the prospect of attracting sex demons. Even though it sounds bizarre, and perhaps impossible, these demon entities are actually capable of physical, even sexual, interaction with these individuals. The demons appear in male and female forms, called *incubi* and *succubi*.

These individuals often learn the hard way that, once embraced, these demons can turn into assailants, forcibly attacking their hosts sexually when they discern that the people are weak or willing.

Though the topic is bizarre, it is a reality that we must be prepared to face as people of diverse background and experience come into the Body of Christ. I have personally ministered to men and women who have been forcibly raped by succubi and incubi. I encountered one young man who confessed numerous rough homosexual episodes with an incubus.

As the fascination with the antichrist spirit of vampirism grows, many deliverance ministers are finding that complaints of incubi and succubi encounters are becoming more common. The victims bear the evidence of being worn out by antichrist spirits. The molested express tearful emotions when finally finding someone who believes their stories and can offer liberation.

Diagnosing Antichrist Spirits

Most any type of demon can be an antichrist spirit. They can often be detected by accusatory statements charging God, the Church and Christians for disappointments in life. Antichrist demons mock, belittle, discredit and smirk at quoted verses and all that believers hold true. When I suspect their presence during deliverance ministry, but it is not obvious, I ask counselees questions about basic Christian concepts. "What do you think about the story of Noah's flood? What is the first thought that comes to your mind when I mention the blood of Jesus and His resurrection?" If the answers are "It's stupid; I hate it; it's impossible," I shift gears by commanding the antichrist spirits out.

An example would be, "You antichrist spirit of mental fatigue, come out. I command this antichrist spirit that hates the atonement to leave now in Jesus' name." On many occasions, I simply address the spirit as an antichrist spirit and tell it to leave. Most of the time that brings relief as the Holy Spirit knows what I am referring to and so does the targeted demon.

Former Muslims frequently need special attention to be cleansed of anti-Christian doctrines. The antichrist precepts of Islam were drilled into them during their school years. Islamic clerics made them recite Koranic verses and passages from the Hadiths over and over. Some need to be deprogrammed. The best way to do so is to ask them questions about the six basic doctrines of the Christian faith that are found in Hebrews 6:1–3. If they give Islamic answers, confidently counter with verses from the Bible.

Battle Offensives for Your Future

The Lord's Prayer instructs us to pray for deliverance from evil. One of the ways to do so is to take the initiative through offensive maneuvers against the enemy. The Bible promises that Satan will flee from those who resist him. One of the most aggressive forms of resistance is to expel demons from those inhabited by them.

With a great revival on the way, many who come into the Kingdom of God will need deliverance from evil spirits. The battle objective for all believers is to get as many people as possible into faith in Christ before the emergence of the Antichrist.

Reading this book has familiarized you with the various types of bondage from which people commonly need liberation. You have learned the dangers and ramifications of involvement with the occult, curses and vows. You have learned how demons complicate relationships, dole out misery through physical and emotional sickness, and invoke heartaches through enslaving addictions.

You have also become acquainted with ramifications of the vampire phenomenon. It is very likely that in the future you will encounter people who have been plagued by demonic molestations as a result of their fascination with vampirism. Among those people, you will no doubt discover many who want to believe God loves them and has plans for their lives. They will be ashamed of their history of inviting demonic sexual attentions, and desperate to be free of the attacks that have resulted.

The love of God extended through you can help the most diabolical of sinners understand the great eternal truth—that Jesus Christ is always willing to offer His cleansing and purity for the shame of their guilt.

Even as you have been set free, so you can be God's instrument of mercy that puts demons to flight from others. No matter how powerful the manifestation, the truth is the same: Demons are subject to the power of Jesus' name.

In this final chapter, we will view guidelines to help you as God leads you to help others be delivered.

21

Guidelines for Helping Others

This chapter outlines how I minister to others in deliverance sessions. Much of what I do has been learned from mentors; it is scriptural, I believe, and important to emulate the methods and styles of those who are experienced in ministry. As you mature in your own experience of ministry, the Holy Spirit will help you to discover the style most effective for you.

Essential Equipping

In deliverance, as with any other aspect of ministry, it is important to learn to become a good listener who is attentive to body language. My objective during interviews is to observe a person's entire personality. It helps me detect demonic issues beyond those that may have prompted the person to come to me.

Voice inflections can expose anger, frustration or pride. Lost words and incoherent speech can be indicative of spirits of forgetfulness, mental disorder and insomnia. Averting the eyes often indicates the presence of shame. People who constantly move their eyes sideways may be struggling with deception and double-mindedness. Those who wring their hands might be struggling with worry and fearfulness. People who constantly lean forward as they speak are at times harboring tendencies to be controlling. The stubborn and the defensive frequently lean back with folded arms and their legs crossed at the ankles. While these may be simply indicators of human expression, it is also possible that the individual can be hosting any one of these particular spirits.

Body language indicators are not scientifically verifiable or universally applicable, but they can prove to be helpful in ministry. I would encourage you not only to be observant, but also to trust the Holy Spirit to guide you and help you cultivate your own methodology of observing what people are expressing through body language.

Revelatory Gifts

There are three revelatory gifts of the Spirit that are basic for ministering deliverance. Those gifts are discerning of spirits, words of knowledge and words of wisdom. God gives revelations to us personally by way of our inner spirit in the way of an impression or sensation. These revelations can come to us as mental pictures and images, specific words that come to mind, and sensations in our bodies. These impressions might also register as feelings or emotions.

Perhaps the best way to describe the process is that God's thoughts and His voice are generally mingled with our own inner thoughts and voices. In other words, impressions from the Lord may seem similar to what we would normally think or feel. But revelations from the Lord have a quality that distinguishes them from our normal thoughts and feelings, making it clear they are inspired by the Holy Spirit.

Here are a couple of examples of how the revelatory gifts might work. As you pray for someone, you suddenly start to feel angry, nervous or lustful. As you examine these feelings, you know the sensations are not pertinent to you. What you are sensing could likely be indicative of corresponding spirits the person you are counseling is hosting.

Or let's say that you have a mental picture of a bathroom cabinet filled with prescription bottles. You know that it is not your bathroom cabinet. The Lord is possibly giving you a word of knowledge that the person may be hiding a problem with prescription drugs.

Or let's say that while the person is talking about matters seemingly unconnected to child rearing, you inwardly hear a child crying. What you have heard might be a word of wisdom indicating that this parent needs to apologize to his or her child for dealing too harshly, or at least the parent needs to confess this behavior before the Lord. Sometimes these sensations indicate something a person must take care of first in order to receive full deliverance.

Preparatory Information

I generally begin a deliverance session with prayer asking for the Lord's guidance.

I usually set aside ample time, sometimes as much as 45 minutes, to ask questions and allow the individuals to describe the problems they are facing. I ask if they are familiar with deliverance, and, if not, I provide a brief explanation about what demons are and what they can do. I have found that referring to invisible evil spirits as "uninvited passengers" can sometimes lessen the shock a person might feel at the thought of being susceptible to demonic forces. I also encourage them with testimonies of how others have gotten free from problems similar to theirs.

At some point, I discuss topics of occult involvement, curses and vows. I talk with them about severing any soul ties. I always mention the necessity of forgiving all who have wronged them.

A portion of my presentation is dedicated to demythologizing stereotypes of long and difficult exorcisms. I make every attempt to help the individuals know what to expect when undergoing deliverance. I tell them about possible manifestations such as gagging, coughing, dizziness and also the inner lifting sensation they might feel as demons are expelled. I also prepare them for the fact that demons are known to speak at times through people, and that what they say may be surprising.

While I downplay the potential, I also let them know that sometimes when demons are expelled it is not uncommon for mucus or vomit to be expelled. I assure them that if strong manifestations do occur, they will be momentary, and the person will be able to regain composure. I make it clear to them that the power of God within us and the spiritual authority we possess is stronger than any invisible enemy.

Words of Encouragement

Before going into the actual deliverance, I give some introductory comments like the ones that follow about how I will minister to them.

"I will begin by leading you in a confession of the Lordship of Christ and what the blood of Jesus has accomplished for you. I'll ask you to name and to forgive those with whom you have unforgiveness issues. Then we will sever any suspected soul ties with manipulators or former lovers or both. I'll have you name them, and then we'll pray that the negative images within your soul will be shattered by the hammer of God's Word. I'll lead you in renouncing any curses and vows.

"I've listened carefully as you have spoken. What you have stated leads me to believe that spirits of X, Y and Z need to be expelled from you. But I recognize that the gift of discerning of spirits can be very subjective, and may not be entirely accurate. The names of the spirits that I call out are based on combinations of what you've said, discernment that I'm exercising, as well as years of experience in dealing with similar situations. Even so, I'll likely be on-target with some named spirits and off target with others. It's somewhat like shooting a shotgun at skeet clays. Some pellets hit the mark and others fall to the ground. There is no need to be concerned about off-target word 'pellets.' The important fact is that God is in control. He will enable me to strike home on the spirits that are in you, and they will come out.

"Whenever I name a spirit that resonates as one that torments you, it's a good step to make it clear that you're setting your will against it. You can do so by giving several exhaling huffs to expel it. Normally, demons come out through the mouth. For this reason, I ask that you refrain from articulating prayers. Keeping your mouth preoccupied with speech can prevent demons from making their exit. Simply pray inwardly and trust the Lord to use me as you huff the spirits out."

The Matter of Manifestations

I continue by helping the individuals know what to expect.

"It is possible that you might experience one or more of the manifestations that I have mentioned. If you begin to hack or cough, I have tissues available. If a spirit tries to speak through your lips or cause you to move physically, know that you have the power to stop the manifestations. I will also apply the authority and Word of God to stop any of those manifestations and to quiet all opposition to what we are trying to accomplish, which is your complete freedom. We have complete authority to make demons stop doing whatever they may try to do, so don't be worried.

"I also want you to know that whatever happens in ministry today is confidential. In the future, I promise not to think of you in terms of what takes place, or to relate to you on the basis of some manifestation that a demon exhibited through you. That's all part of the process, and it's normal, so don't worry about it. Just get free.

"Your freedom in Christ is my sole objective. The evidence that you have been set free is that there will be a noticeable change in your emotions and behavior.

"Have you understood my explanations and the format your deliverance will take? Do you have any questions? Do you understand that I'm not a licensed counselor or a mental health professional and that my ministry is faith-based? On the basis of all I have shared in preparation for this moment, do you want to proceed?"

Deliverance Begins

If the persons answer in the affirmative, then I begin the process of the deliverance ministry. In some instances, I use the technique I described earlier in chapter 13, "Obliterating Demonic Strongholds in Your Mind." I will ask them to recall the most recent incident of their most troublesome issue. I then ask them to hold those feelings and to trace back to the first time they experienced those emotions. I then ask them what those feelings made them believe about themselves that is contrary to God's Word and a wholesome self-image. Most often the self-image they express is based on a satanically inspired lie.

I then ask if they would like for the Lord to give them His perspective on both them and the event. The majority of the time, Jesus speaks words of consolation and encouragement into the person's mind. Occasionally, the Lord admonishes them that it is time to be rid of a sinful problem. Whatever the case, armed with Jesus' true perspective on the situation, I command the evil spirit to leave. The results are almost always very positive and satisfying.

We continue in this manner and with the other approaches to deliverance until it is obvious that the persons have received freedom and relief.

Ending the Session

At the completion of the ministry, I ask how they are doing. If the report is that they are still sensing something, we continue on in ministry. If the report is that they feel relief and peace inside, I encourage them to take a few moments to offer up enthusiastic praise and thanksgiving for what the Lord has done.

I then charge the persons to keep reasonable disciplines of prayer and Bible study, and to maintain fellowship with strong believers. I encourage the newly delivered persons to stay in contact to give me updates on their progress. Afterward, I close the session by committing the persons to the Lord in prayer.

All in all, it is a wonderful process and a marvelous experience to help dear people who have been bound by the enemy step into newfound freedom and vitality. And it is a great privilege to be used by the Lord in leading people into such a degree of release through the God-given means of deliverance. What a joy to partner with Jesus in His ministry of liberating the captives!

The Epilogue includes a challenge and an invitation for you to join the company of the Lord's servant warriors who participate in setting the captives free. At salvation, you were automatically enlisted in His army. Those whom He has enlisted are called into service for Him in some capacity that reflects the life and ministry of Jesus Christ.

Well-informed deliverance commandos are in short supply. My hope is that as you have read this book, you have received some helpful encouragement in understanding the various aspects of the ministry of deliverance. Armed with this knowledge, it may well be time for you to begin some hands-on training. The Epilogue will close with your prayer of commitment to step into the arena and begin to minister to others.

Epilogue

The Challenge of Commitment

From the time I began writing this book, I have sensed a weight pressing upon me to move forward with this project. I am convinced that what I have felt carries implications for many who read it. The weight has been an awareness of not only God's pleasure, but also His divine sense of responsibility that this work be completed.

You might ask, "What does that have to do with me? How does Jim Croft's sense of the weight of God's pleasure and divine responsibility apply to me?"

The fact that you have read this book is not coincidental. I believe you were divinely destined to do so. Perhaps, as you have read the contents, thoughts of your own calling have stirred in your spirit. I am speaking of a calling from the Lord to become a warrior in God's strike force against the powers of darkness that have arisen as this age draws to a close.

My hope is that you also sense the weight of God's pleasure and divine responsibility to be involved in the deliverance ministry. I believe this book has equipped you with many insights you will need. Of all the diverse ministry experiences I have had, I would have to testify that setting the captives free has remained the most gratifying of all. Great sermons can fade from people's memories. Prayers for the sick may or may not work. But deliverance is distinctive. More often than not, it brings instantaneous changes for the better to the lives of those who experience it.

Throughout the years, I have ministered to thousands of hurting people who had demons residing within. To this day, I am still moved to tears when a captive is liberated. There are few joys that equal seeing the smiles and laughter of those who know the power of shameful bondages has been broken in their lives and they have been set free.

Time to Pray

It is my hope and prayer that this book has inspired you to become a liberated liberator. If so, I encourage you to embrace that challenge by reciting this closing prayer of commitment:

Father God, I want to participate in Your will as it is accomplished on earth as it is in heaven. The souls and bodies of mankind are designed to be Your habitation in the Holy Spirit. Too many people are tormented by uninvited and invisible wicked spirits. For Your will to be done, those demons must be displaced by the majestic presence of Your only begotten Son.

Under the guidance of the Holy Spirit and in the authority of the Word of God, I commit myself to follow Jesus' command. With Your help and by Your power, it is my intention to expel evil spirits from people's lives. Lord, I ask for You to anoint me for my appointed destiny of setting the captives free. In Jesus' name, Amen.

# Appendix

Ministry Resource Guide

The ministers on this list are experienced in deliverance ministry. Their styles are based upon the way the Holy Spirit has led as their ministry processes and techniques matured. In some instances, their methods will differ with those presented in this book. The variations are in keeping with the biblical concept that every believer has a unique calling.

Alabama

Susan Bowman
The Pool Ministries
P.O. Box 40507
Tuscaloosa, Alabama
www.thepoolministries.org

California

Shelby and Sandi Rogers
Davis, California
530-758-0893
sandi_rogers@sbcglobal.net

Florida

Jim Croft
Boca Raton, Florida
561-703-7829
jcm888@comcast.net
www.thoughtsfromjim.com

James Bethea
Palm Beach Gardens, Florida
kimo@spirit-and-life.org
www.spirit-and-life.org

Dave and Linda Ward
Delray Beach, Florida
Shepherdea@bellsouth.net

Seby Matacena
Miami, Florida
305-316-8696
smatacena@gmail.com

William Bender
Tampa, Florida
info@AnothenLife.org
www.AnothenLife.org
www.LinkedIn.com/in/billbender

Georgia

Jim Hodgin
Conyers, Georgia
770-841-8967
hodginhotel@juno.com

Missouri

Dick and Donna Sorenson
Church on the Rock
5110 Brookhart Drive
Harrisonville, MO 64701
www.rockharrisonville.com
816-380-2428

North Carolina

Janice Maynor and Juanita Frierson
Teshuwah Ministries
Outreach of Cornerstone Fellowship
P.O. Box 456
Pineville, NC 28134
Church: 704-889-4673
Cell: 704-962-5251
teshuwah@carolina.rr.com

Derek Prince Ministries
Charlotte, North Carolina
704-357-3556
www.derekprince.com

Index

Adam, 58, 59, 60, 61, 180, 182, 195
adultery, 33, 85, 105, 166
  spiritual adultery, 81, 86, 89–92,
    93, 106
Alexander the Great, 57
angels
evil/fallen angels, 51–52, 54–55, 56,
  57, 58, 59, 60
angels of God, 48, 53, 56, 57, 58
antichrist, 131, 204
antichrist, spirits of, 209–10
  battle offensives against, 216–17
  diagnosing of, 215–16
  effects of exposure to, 211
  in the United States, 210, 211
  vast number and types of, 210–11
  See also Islam, antichrist spirit of;
    vampirism, antichrist spirit of
Antiquities of the Jews (Josephus), 77
Aratus, 130–31
astrology, 88, 89–90
Athens, 130

Balaam, 126–27
Balak, 126–27
baptism, 169
  baptismal vows, 164–65
  in the Holy Spirit, 36, 45

infant baptism, 165
  by water, 65, 68, 113, 135, 137–39,
    185
Basham, Don, 55
Becky, testimony and liberation of,
  156–57
Body of Christ, the, 187
  biblical practices for, 135
  and revelation, 129–30

Campus Crusade for Christ, 44
chaff. *See* ministry chaff, areas of
communion. *See* Lord's Supper, the
Coptic Christians, 212
Christian homes and families
  demonic attacks on, 195
  expelling of demonic home wreck-
    ers, 200
  skewed perspectives concerning
    spiritual and home life, 196–97
  solutions for problems and hard-
    ships in family life, 199–200
  ways in which demons create family
    disharmony, 197–98
Christianity, 140, 184, 209, 212
  mockery of, 213–14
Christians, 63–64, 100, 129, 130,
  132, 168

and biblical protocol regarding evangelization of, 68
Coptic Christians, 212
deception of, 118
denial of the power of grace by, 204–5
divorce rate among, 165
and facing the pressures of antichrist spirits, 210
and fleeing from idolatry (the Christians of Ephesus), 95–96
susceptibility of to demons (demonic infestation), 67–68, 69–70
Croft, Holly, 23–24
evil spirits as the cause of illness in, 24–25
expulsion of demons from, 25–26
health issues of, 24
stubbornness of, 24, 26
Croft, Jim, 24, 25, 119–21, 161
affliction of by evil spirits, 32–34, 40, 47–49
calling of as a "Bible teacher," 37–38
childhood of, 64–65, 154–55
confidence of in God's love, 48
deliverance of from specific evil spirits, 39–40
fasting of, 47
friendship with Derek Prince, 46
hallucinations of, 47, 48–49
influence of Derek Prince on, 43, 44
insecurities of, 47
intolerance/hatred of his parents by, 66, 67
introduction of to the topic of demons, 29–31
and the Lord's voice, 149–50
ministry of, 46
rebaptism of, 47
rebellion of, 32, 67
supernatural encounter of with the Spirit of God, 65–66
thankfulness of, 40–41
use of tobacco by, 150–51, 152–53

vision of the Arabian horse and the Trainer, 151–52
and the weight of God's pleasure and divine responsibility, 227–28
Croft, Kari, 23, 24
Croft, Prudence, 23, 24, 25, 35, 41, 161
abuse of, 43
shyness of, 43
Croft, Rachel, 35
Croft, Sharon, 23, 24
cross, the, as symbol of the sacrificial death of Christ, 214
culture
American, 79
Jewish, 79
curanderoism, 88
curses, 88–89, 92, 97, 98, 99, 101, 102, 106–7, 110, 111, 133, 159, 168, 169, 216, 221, 222
fear of witchcraft curses, 126–27
generational curses, 126–27
See also denouncements; occult practices, and resultant curses

Daniel, and the prince of Persia, 56–57
Darrell, deliverance of from obsessive-compulsive disorder (OCD), 189–91
David, 76
Deliver Us from Evil (Basham), 55
deliverance, 15, 63, 71–73, 148, 202
absolutes and variables concerning, 118–20
"backtracking" technique used in, 155–56
deliverance from iniquity, 206–7
deliverance from sexual perversion, 184–85
deliverance of those with mental conditions, 188–89
deliverance of those with physical conditions, 191–92
ministry of, 26–27
and the "naturally supernatural" approach to, 131–33

See also baptism, by water; deliverance ministry; Jesus, deliverance ministry of; laying on of hands; Lord's Supper, the; prayer cloths; self-deliverance

deliverance ministry, 219, 225
ending deliverance sessions properly, 224
essential equipping for (voice inflection and body language), 219–20
preparatory information for, 221–22
process of, 224
revelatory gifts of the Spirit used in, 220–21
and spirit manifestations, 223
using words of encouragement, 222–23

demonology, 30, 32, 117

demons, 19, 67–68, 180
attacks of on humans, 21
cleverness of, 119
confusing terminology concerning "demon possession," 71
demonic strongholds, 148–49
depiction of different types of, 52, 59
infiltration of demons through the flesh, 85–86
nature of, 60–61
origins of, 57–58
psychological characteristics of, 60–61
reason for their existence, 58–60
residence of in innocent persons, 23
"spin-off" demons, 85
and spiritual adultery, 86
as spiritual parasites, 80
types of, 80–81
types of misery produced by, 21
See also Christian homes and families, demonic attacks on; demons, and human emotions; evil spirits; occult practices, and resultant curses

demons, and human emotions
demons' use of our emotions to access us, 81

demons' use of envy and selfishness, 83
and facing the truth about ourselves, 84–85
the process that demons use to access us, 83–84

denouncements, 161–62
and help for "crop failures," 168–70
Luke's story concerning, 162–64
in parent/child relationships, 162
sample prayer concerning, 170–71

Derek Prince Ministries, 44, 45

Diana, 96

disciples, the, 15, 75

divination, 88, 127

divorce, 165, 166, 169

"dominion mandate," the, 61–62

drunkenness, 85

duwendes, 53–54

Egypt, 212
gross domestic product (GDP) of, 212–13
literacy rate in, 213

Elisha, 102

Epimenides of Knossos, 130, 131

evangelism, 35, 68, 69

Eve, 58, 59, 60, 61, 180, 195

evil spirits, 16, 23, 103, 109, 140
intelligence of, 105
physical signs of an evil spirit leaving the body, 109
restlessness of, 105
skepticism about their existence, 51
as squatters within the bodies of believers, 124
types of in different countries, 52
See also antichrist, spirits of; demons; evil spirits, personal sightings of; infirmities, spirits of

evil spirits, personal sightings of
by Ralph (a Filipino evangelist), 53–54
by Tino (grandson of Jim Croft), 52–53

exorcists, 76–77
ancient Jewish exorcists, 76–78

Ezekiel, 129, 168

forgiveness, 95, 103, 128, 164, 170, 177
  mutual forgiveness, 162, 169
  prayers of forgiveness, 110–11
fornication, 46, 85, 183, 184
free will, 58, 175
freedom, in Christ, 223
freedom, from demons, initial steps to take for, 93
  Step One: discipline, 93–94
  Step Two: repentance, 94–95, 99
  Step Three: deliverance, 95
  Step Four: cleaning one's house of occult items and spirits, 95–100
Full Gospel Business Men's Fellowship International (FGBMFI), 31, 35

Garden of Eden, 59, 61
God, 17, 21, 57, 65–66, 70, 127, 159, 161, 176, 195, 196, 199–200
  affection of, 154
  army of, 209–10
  dwelling place of, 56
  forgiveness of, 95, 103
  goodness and mercy of, 58
  grace of, 40, 133, 192, 204–5
  involvement of with His creation, 58–59
  jealousy of, 95, 168
  justice of, 58
  love of for us that covers our sins, 168–69
  nature of, 149
  omniscience of, 154
  Satan's hatred of, 108
  will of, 107, 167
Gospel in the Stars, The (Seiss), 89
grace, 40, 68, 100, 133, 170, 171, 192
  denial of the power of, 204–5
guilt, 19, 22, 33, 94, 149, 151, 163, 184, 196, 217

heavenlies (the first, second, and third heavens), 55–56
  war in the heavenlies, 56–57
High Point Southern Baptist Church, 36
Holy Spirit, the, 47, 68, 70, 104, 109, 111, 117, 177, 180, 202, 216
  baptism in, 36, 45
  at the Day of Pentecost, 131
  gifts of, 36, 69, 220–21
  help of in our healing, 156
  power of, 26, 32, 141
homosexuality, 47, 85, 181–82, 184
horoscopes, 90, 106

idolatry, 79, 85, 86, 99, 111, 121, 175
  cultural idolatry, 106
  fleeing from, 95–96
incubi, 213, 215
infirmities, spirits of, 187–88
  dealing with spirits of pain, 193–94
  mental infirmities, 188–89
  obsessive-compulsive disorder (OCD), 189–91
  physical infirmities, 191–92
iniquity, 201–2
  deliverance from, 206–7
  deliverance from (Wilbur's story), 202–3
  distinction of from sin, 203–4
  Greek and Hebrew terms for, 204
  iniquity-hardened hearts, 204–6
  and lawlessness, 205
interpersonal relationships, problems common in, 105–6
Iran, 212
Iraq, 212
Islam, antichrist spirit of, 210, 211–13
  stifling effects of Islam on economies and women, 211–12
Israel, 79
  casting out of demons in, 76
  under the Old Covenant, 127
Italy, 212
  gross domestic product (GDP) of, 212

literacy rate in, 212

James, 70, 167
jealousy, 85
Jeremiah, 90
Jesus Christ, 77, 92, 94, 96, 103,
    123, 149, 167, 168, 224, 225
  accomplishment of at Calvary, 169
  casting out of evil spirits by, 15, 19,
    75, 118
  deliverance ministry of, 78–79
  healing ministry of, 187, 192
  Jesus' "41" team of exorcists, 75–76,
    79
    and the laying on of hands by,
      140–41
    as the Light of the World, 214
    ownership of believers by, 17
    as the Passover Lamb, 135
    peaceful ministry of, 16
    power of, 110
    resurrection of, 23
    temptation of, 47
Jesus Movement, 45, 119
Jews, 135
Job, 205
John, 129; on the spirit of error, 81
John the Baptist, 94
Josephus, Flavius, 76–77
Joshua, 206

Kingdom of God, 100
Korah the Levite, 127

laughter, 125
law of Moses, 15
laying on of hands, 140–41, 185
legalism, 22
lewdness, 85
Lewis, C. S., 51
Lord's Supper, the, 135–37, 214
lust, 30, 33, 108

macumba, 88
Malachi, 165
manipulation, 173
  manipulative strategies, 173–74
  spiritual forces employed in,
    174–75

marriage, 34, 80, 81, 105, 108, 164,
    183, 199
marriage vows, 165–67
  vulnerability and authority in, 180
martial arts, 91–92
Masonic lodges, 167
masturbation, 30, 34, 40
Matacena, Seby, 136, 137, 154–54,
    155
mediums, 87–88
Michael the archangel, 56
ministry chaff, areas of, 123
  concern over manifestations,
    124–25
  concern over "shouting out" of
    demons, 125–26
  fear of witchcraft curses, 126–27
  ongoing generational repentance,
    127–29
  rejection of signs and wonders,
    129–31
miracles, 15, 136, 141, 205

Naaman, 102
New Age, Christian concern over,
    129, 130
New Covenant, 95, 127, 136
New Testament, 19, 47, 55, 59, 71,
    80, 131, 179, 204

obsessive-compulsive disorder
    (OCD), 189–91
occult items and spirits, removal of
    from the home, 95–98
  children and the removal of occult
    items, 101
  dealing with family objections to,
    101–2
  helping others to remove occult
    items, 100
  methods used for, 99
occult practices, and resultant curses,
    86–87
  specific curses, 88–89
  specific practices, 87–88
Old Covenant, 95, 127
Old Testament, 86, 95, 131
omens, 87

interpreters of, 88
orisha, 88
Ouija boards, 88, 101, 106

paranormal, the, 86, 90–91, 99
Passover (Paschal) Meal, 135, 136
Paul, 69, 80, 130, 166, 179, 199
  on the spirit of fear, 81
  use of prayer cloths by, 141, 142
  on the works of the flesh, 85
Pentecost, 131
Phaenomena (Aratus), 130–31
Pharisees, 77
Philip the Evangelist, 68
pornography, 46, 79, 105, 108, 200
prayer, 10, 19, 36, 39, 65, 99, 110,
    147, 154, 178, 185, 200, 224, 225,
    228
  of confession and repentance, 70,
    99, 110–11
  for expulsion of demons, 111–12
  healing of marriages with prayer, 29
  for placing desires before the Lord,
    170–71
  for relief from curses, 111
  for those suffering from infirmities,
    188, 191, 193, 202, 203
prayer cloths, 133, 135, 141–43
pride, 22, 104, 181, 201, 202, 203,
    206, 219
Prince, Derek, 31, 35, 45, 55, 66,
    142
  influence of on Jim Croft, 43, 44
Prince, Lydia, 98
principalities, 55, 56

rebellion, 58, 82, 106, 175, 202
  of Israel, 79, 127
  of Satan, 54, 57
redemption, 62, 128–29, 180
repentance, 94–95, 96, 100, 102,
    104, 168, 178, 205, 206
  ongoing generational repentance,
    127–29
  prayers of, 70, 99
  as the precursor to deliverance, 94
role-playing games, 101, 106

Roman Catholic Church, 137, 164,
    212

salvation, 68, 69, 126, 128, 133, 183,
    201, 204, 225
sanctification, 159
Santeria, 88
Satan/Lucifer, 51, 58, 59, 60, 175,
    176
  armor of, 148–49
  attacks of on human relationships
    and families, 195, 197–98
  cleverness of, 119
  hatred of God by, 108
  pride and iniquity of, 201–2
  rage of, 209
  rebellion of, 54, 57
  renunciation of, 137
  role of in perverse sexual acts, 180,
    183
  rulership of, 55
  the Satanic phrase "I will," 206
  warfare of at the end of time,
    209–10
  See also Satan's kingdom, structure
    of
Satan's kingdom, structure of, 54–55
  locations under siege, 55–56
  military hierarchy of, 55
Saul, 89
Screwtape Letters, The (Lewis), 51
séances, 88, 101, 106
self-deliverance, 103–4
  experiencing deliverance, 108–10
  from addiction issues, 104–5
  from curses, 106
  from mental issues, 107–8
  from the occult, 106
  from problems in interpersonal rela-
    tionships, 105–6
  from sexual issues, 108
  motivation for, 104
  process of, 110–12
Seiss, Joseph A., 89
sex/sexuality, 108
  deliverance from sexual perversion,
    184–85

oral sex, 181
origins of sexual perversity, 180–82
premarital sex, 108
sex addictions, 182
sexual dysfunction, 166
what sex symbolizes, 108
See also homosexuality; lust; masturbation; pornography
sin, 59, 60, 96, 103, 107, 128, 153, 184, 206
Greek term for, 204
guilt concerning, 22, 149, 151
and rebellion, 181
sin contributing to the entrance of demons in our lives, 23, 49
See also iniquity; repentance; sex/sexuality, origins of sexual perversity
Solomon, 76–77, 175, 199
soothsayers, 87
sorcerers, 87
sorcery, 85, 97, 126
soul ties, 145, 175–76
identifying soul ties, 176–77
severing soul ties, 171, 177–78, 221, 222
Spain, 212
gross domestic product (GDP) of, 213
literacy rate in, 213
spiritual "umbilical cords," 175, 176, 177
spiritual warfare, 9, 10, 11, 45, 117, 153, 209
strongholds, 145, 150, 153, 154
demonic strongholds, 148–49, 155
mental strongholds, 147
misinformation strongholds, 155, 157
self-deliverance from strongholds, 158
succubi, 213, 215
Syria, 212

"Tale of Two Sisters, A," 90–91
Tarot cards, 88
tobacco, use of, 85, 150–51
Torah, the, 79
truth, 83, 112, 217
biblical truth, 117, 118, 119, 128, 211
facing the truth about ourselves, 84–85
progressive nature of, 123
Turkey, 212
gross domestic product (GDP) of, 212
literacy rate in, 212

vampirism, antichrist spirit of, 213
vampires and sexual fantasies, 214–15
vampirism as mockery and repudiation of sacred beliefs, 213–14
VanHoozier, Don, 35, 37, 38–39, 48
prayers of for Jim Croft, 39–40
voodoo, 88
vows, 70, 145, 159, 161–62, 169, 171, 216, 221, 222
baptismal vows, 138
ill-advised vows, 167–68, 169–70
marriage vows, 34, 169
See also vows, breaking of
vows, breaking of, 164
of baptismal vows, 164–65, 169
of marriage vows, 165–67

War in Heaven (D. Prince), 55
"what if" questions, 49–50
Wilbur, deliverance of from iniquity, 202–3
witchcraft, 87, 97, 106, 174–75, 176
fear of witchcraft curses, 126–27
spirits of witchcraft, 22, 142, 143

yoga, 91, 99

Zeus, 131

Jim Croft, who is recognized for a notable ministry of healing and deliverance, delights in inspiring laypeople to discover their spiritual callings and in serving as a pastor to pastors. He has ministered in more than thirty nations, and his published works have been translated into numerous languages.

Jim has served as a board member of Derek Prince Ministries since its inception. He is recognized as a bishop of the Flock of Christ Mission's network of churches in Nigeria, with approximately 150,000 members. He was instrumental in the foundational years of Faith Church of Budapest, Hungary, which currently has 70,000 members. Jim is considered an expert on Islamic issues and assists several ministries to Muslims. He has received numerous civic awards from Israeli Jewish service organizations for his various contributions.

Jim pastors Gold Coast Christian Church of Boca Raton, Florida. He and his wife, Prudence, have four happily married daughters who are devoted to the purposes of Christ.

Jim Croft may be contacted for speaking engagements. He can be reached at jcm888@comcast.net or by calling 561-703-7829. For more of Jim's teachings and itinerary go to www.thoughtsfromjim.com.